*A Compost of*
# SECRETS

---

IAN EDWARDS

Published by I C Edwards

Copyright © 2023. All rights reserved. No portion of this publication may be used, reproduced or transmitted by any means, digital, electronic, mechanical, photocopy or recording without written permission of the publisher, except in the case of brief quotations within critical articles or reviews.

ISBN: 978-0-6488057-2-4 (paperback)
ISBN: 978-0-6488057-3-1 (e-book)

First edition, 2023

Cover design by Danica Gacesa McLean and Anne Edwards. Artwork by Anne Edwards.

The cover makes use of an applique technique. It contains elements of the Japanese art of Sashiko in which old materials are recycled and embroidered in order to create something new.

The scraps which have been sewn together represent the way in which in we recall our lives. Our memories are reservoirs of past experience. We remember and reassemble them according to the meanings we have attributed to each.

For book orders and enquiries,
contact: anneandiane@hotmail.com

 A catalogue record for this book is available from the National Library of Australia

For my friend, Joan

# The Port Adelaide
# Of Ruth Fewster

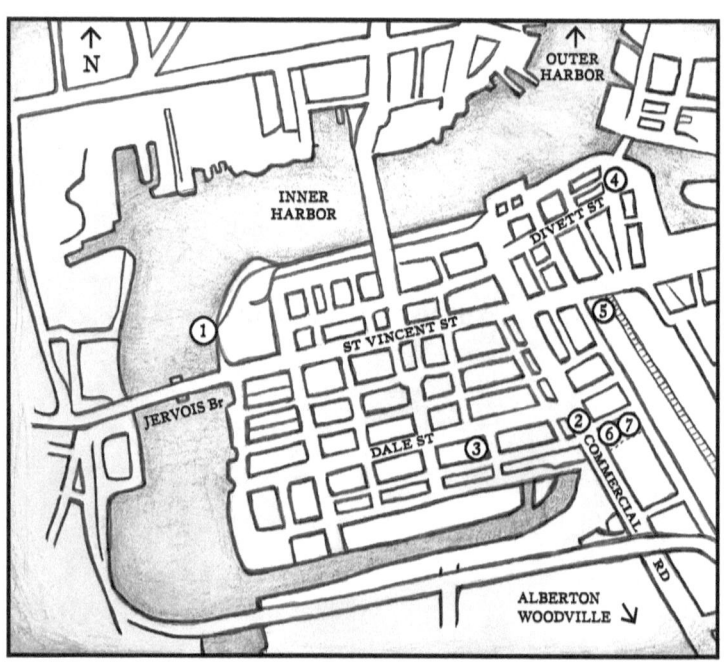

1. The Inverlass (1929-1934)
2. Fewster Residence (1937-1955)
3. Port Adelaide Methodist Church
4. Port Carriers
5. Port Dock Railway Station
6. Port Adelaide Uniting Church
7. The Bent Pine Community Garden

# Table of Contents

**Prologue** ................................................................................. 1

**Chapter One**
Port Adelaide 1935 — The First Secret ....................................... 6

**Chapter Two**
Alberton 2015 — The First Conversation ................................. 24

**Chapter Three**
Port Districts 1936-1954 — Making our Way ......................... 31

**Chapter Four**
Retreat to the Garden ............................................................. 48

**Chapter Five**
Port Adelaide 1945-1960 — Working and Waiting ................. 58

**Chapter Six**
Port Adelaide 1960-1982 — The Second Secret ....................... 75

**Chapter Seven**
The First Garden Story ............................................................ 93

**Chapter Eight**
Cheltenham 1984-2010 — Passings ........................................ 103

**Chapter Nine**
The End of Worlds ................................................................. 114

**Chapter Ten**
Wimereux, France 1916 — Poem from the Trenches ............. 129

**Chapter Eleven**
Yorke Peninsula 1923 — Lilac and Rocks .............................. 139

**Chapter Twelve**
Port Adelaide 1949 — 'The Dinner' Revisited ....................... 153

**Chapter Thirteen**
Cheltenham 2021 — The Third Secret .................................. 167

**Chapter Fourteen**
The Bent Pine Compost ......................................................... 175

**Chapter Fifteen**
The Book of Ruth .................................................................. 179

**Epilogue** .............................................................................. 191

**Author's note** ..................................................................... 199

**Sources** ............................................................................... 200

**Acknowledgements** ............................................................ 203

*So God expelled them from the Garden of Eden
and sent them to work the ground,
the same dirt out of which they'd been made.*

Genesis 3:23

# Prologue

About that day, this is what I remember: waking up on my mother's lap wrapped in a grey blanket, her susurrant 'shh-shhs' coaxing me back to a fitful sleep.

This is what I don't remember: Father climbing a shifting rope ladder, one-handed, out of the deep hold of the *Inverlass*, my limp body cradled upon his shoulder.

And this I don't *have* to remember, for it has never left me: it was the day Father disappeared from our lives.

I was six years old then. I am ninety-three now. In recent years, I have been interviewed a few times about my life. There was the one with our local paper, the *Messenger*, which was to promote an exhibition at the Maritime Museum that featured our family's life on board the *Inverlass* in the early 1930s. Another piece with the Port Adelaide Central Mission was to help celebrate its 100th anniversary.

The Mission has been the social arm of the Methodist church for a century. I was just a baby when my mum first carried me into church and I've been connected to the Mission ever since. It was so important for us to be part of the

Mission — to feel that we were doing something good in the world. Since I was four years old and attended the free kindergarten set up for disadvantaged children, until now when I still knit blankets for young people living in their 24-Hour House, I have endeavoured to contribute to the work.

The church and the local community in the Port have kept my life on track, like two rail lines, providing me with direction and stability. I have been on this track for ninety years and am myself, I suppose, part of the social history of the Port.

'Ruth,' people say to me, 'you're amazing for your age!' It is a compliment often given to old people — patronising sometimes. I have to say though that I do retain certain abilities. These are not so much related to my physical mobility — I am prone to falls — nor to the robustness of my overall health — I, too, have my share of medical appointments. No, I am fortunate because I have maintained the ability to carefully listen to others and the detail of what they are saying. Furthermore, I reflect upon what I hear, passing it through the filters of what I have previously known or understood. It is called learning. I am grateful that I have retained this capability because learning can lead to change. And there are so many changes that impose themselves on a nonagenarian, many of them, if not most, unwelcome; the idea that I can still *choose* to change is very important to me.

For us 'oldies', memories are a refuge of sorts against the rising sense of our mortality. And yet, what now requires my attention is to be found in the spaces of my life where neither memory nor explanation exist.

'Why would you bother doing this at your age?' you might ask.

And I would reply, 'It started with a congenial luncheon at my local football club and became an adventure upon which I willingly embarked.'

I would find out that buried family secrets, despite their quiescence, do not die entirely. They merely compost over the decades, becoming part of a soil which produces new consequences for old decisions.

Todd Brown stood looking at the cascade of nasturtiums escaping the retaining wall that bordered the old tennis court. He was in the community garden at the back of the Port Adelaide Church. Caught by the early morning sun, the nasturtiums' yellow and orange flowers flowed over and down the retaining wall like molten lava. The image pleased Todd. His four-year-old granddaughter knew the word lava and used it to dramatic effect in a game they currently played. Certain parts of the floor were 'no-go' areas (lava) and the task was to find a way from one room of the house to another, usually via safe islands of rugs or furniture. She managed this better than he did, aided by her self-nominated authority to announce new safe havens whenever things got tricky.

This large area at the back of the church was originally a place of stables and sheds and then quite a bit later — sometime in the 1960s — a large chunk of it was bituminised and turned into a tennis court. Playing on the old bitumen tennis court in midsummer would, at times, have felt like stepping on lava. Now, in 2020, it was surrounded by green: vegetable plots, raised garden beds, an expanse of lawn and a stand of mature plane trees that provided deep shade in summer. It had become a place of coolness and retreat. Todd wasn't much of a gardener. Never had been, really. His interest had been sparked a year or so earlier on a Saturday morning at a free public presentation at the Strathalbyn Library. 'Strath' is a town about fifty-five kilometres south east of Adelaide. The session which he and his partner Eva attended was to announce a movement called 'Grow Free'. Andrew, a young man with a luxuriant beard which looked as if it had been grown with the help of a good quality potting mix, talked about the disconnect between food production and people.

There was an alienation, Andrew explained, between production and consumption which meant that many people did not have ready access to fresh and healthy green produce, especially those who were not well-off. He suggested that we each had more capacity to grow vegetables and fruit than we realised. We only needed to support each other more effectively to do so and be willing to be generous with our neighbours and local community in that process. They had started placing carts outside of houses, shops, churches, almost any place really, upon which fresh produce was left and picked up. The words 'Take what you need and give what you can' adorned each cart. They were seeking to expand this network of carts and trolleys around the towns and suburbs. A fundamental principle of Grow Free was to 'give without expecting anything in return' and the greater aim was to nurture a healthier and more caring community.

After the talk, and upon exiting the building, Todd and his partner Eva looked at each other somewhat telepathically, until one voiced the question: 'Did we just hear the gospel?' They agreed they had but not as any kind of religious proclamation. It was simply a proclamation of 'good'.

Todd and Eva were inspired that day to start a community garden on the vacant land at the back of their church. It had been a good decision. However, what puzzled — no, what troubled Todd was the notion that if he had been so struck by having heard the 'gospel' proclaimed that day in Strathalbyn, why did this also evoke a feeling that he had not heard the gospel proclaimed in his church in the previous few years?

As an observation, it was unfair — blatantly so. He knew that. But he had to own it — it was how he felt — and, more importantly, he had to figure out why he felt that way. There were good friends, creative and gifted people, whom he respected and cared for that were part of this place. Nevertheless, he was beginning to understand how the end of a long marriage must feel.

CHAPTER ONE

# Port Adelaide 1935 — The First Secret

Every Saturday night we had to have a bath. After mine, Mum would braid my hair into tiny plaits all over. In the morning, untied and set free, each one would be squiggly and I would have glorious curls. They were ready for Sunday which was a day spent going to church. We went to worship more than once. Father was superintendent of the Sunday school and sang in the choir. We kids also attended Sunday school. We weren't allowed to do much else on a Sunday. We were quite a religious family. Even though we lived on a ship, it was a sin to swim on Sunday.

One Saturday night, Mum was doing my hair and we heard a commotion on the deck above us. Father was out. He was usually out because he was in the Lodge. He joined the Lodge because he thought that Lodge people were supposed to help each other with jobs and that sort of thing.

## PORT ADELAIDE 1935 — THE FIRST SECRET

It didn't really happen. It was the time of the Great Depression. Most people were living hand-to-mouth.

As Mum worked on my hair, the ruckus continued. She stopped, hands and fingers suspended above my head, and we listened. We were petrified. The hatches were latched of course but they weren't lockable. A ship's best security in Port was to pull up the gangway but ours rarely was. We often had at least one, sometimes two, other boats sharing the same mooring, and our neighbours had to cross our vessel to get to their own from the wharf. But this noise was different to the usual footfall of neighbours.

The screeching of our pet galah on the deck above us suddenly ceased. That was ominous. Aunt Josie was staying with us, and she herded my sister and two brothers to the dining room. Mum hustled me off the stool and brought me there, too, as though it was a designated place of last refuge. In the subdued light of a lantern, we stood together, hushed and with wondering eyes, as if we were part of a nativity scene. Except for Mum. She took Father's revolver and stood by the latched cabin door. Having lived some years on the farm she had some familiarity with the use of guns. But that was with sick or injured farm animals or with wildlife, not with humans.

Thankfully, it didn't get to the point of her having to point the gun at anyone. The commotion above stopped as suddenly as it had begun and, in the dining room, conversation began to bubble between us, at first cautiously and then frenetically, like a cooking pot that is just coming to the boil.

We don't know what caused the burglars to leave. We had no phone or radio on board. Someone must have seen them rummaging through gear and equipment on deck and called the police. The perpetrators, two sailors from a foreign vessel due to leave port the following day, were apprehended and taken into custody. They had been drinking at one of the nearby hotels and hatched their plan *under the influence*, as they say. Some of Father's tools were in their possession.

Mum was mortified by the summons issued afterwards by the police. She would have to go to court and make public statements about what took place that evening. Reluctantly she went. She survived the experience of being a witness in an open court, but from what we could tell, it was no less an ordeal for her than the robbery itself. That was Mum: so strong and courageous on the one hand and so self-doubting on the other. Our pet galah, who had been the lone sentry on deck that evening, did not survive the affair.

While in many respects, we Fewsters were an average family living in Port Adelaide in the early 1930s, *where* we lived was not average at all. Our house was a coal hulk. A coal hulk was a ship that was, essentially, a floating storage bin. Steam had long supplanted sail in commercial maritime shipping and steam engines required coal. A small number of ships regarded as too old or uneconomical for further service on the open ocean maintained at least part of their previous identity and became coal suppliers to other ships in port.

Bert and Mabel Fewster had four kids; two boys and two girls. From oldest to youngest, they were Evelyn, Reg, Trevor and me, Ruth. The *Inverlass* was the name of the ship we lived on. It was an old windjammer that once plied the ocean routes between Europe and Australia with, depending on the winds, fifteen sails billowing on three masts. Now it sailed no more. Instead, it was towed like a barge up and down the Port River to retrieve or deliver its cargo. Given its description as a coal hulk, the *Inverlass* was even more unique as our cargo was grain and not coal.

The *Inverlass* was owned by the Barley Board of South Australia, and in 1930, our father was appointed as its caretaker. The Barley Board installed a grain grading plant on the *Inverlass* which employed twenty-four men when it was operating at full capacity. The price of barley was very low during the Great Depression. The company would purchase low-grade grain and, by passing it through the machinery installed on board, they would extract the higher quality grain from the rest and store it in the hold of the ship. It was a sort of gleaning process. The grain was mostly barley which was then bagged, stored in the hold, and ultimately sold on at profit. When they had an order, a ship would tie up alongside the *Inverlass* and the grain was off-loaded from one vessel to the other, either onto the *Inverlass* for milling or off it for export. At other times, the *Inverlass* was towed by barge or tug to the receiving ship for unloading which meant that our home would be temporarily moored some distance from our usual berth down near the Jervois Bridge in the inner harbour.

The Jervois Bridge was a swing bridge which joined Port Adelaide to Glanville, Semaphore and the Peninsula. It opened for the benefit of the ketches and barques wanting to tie up in the Portland Canal further south. To create passage, the span swung outwards over the water rather than being lifted above it. This was not without problems. If the weather got too hot, the metal would expand. Then the bridge wouldn't close properly, leaving traffic, especially cars, trains and buses, stranded. Some intrepid pedestrians and cyclists were able to successfully make the jump between the proximal parts of the bridge. The rest would have to wait for a fire engine to spray the metal spans with cold water to shrink them. Sometimes a tug boat would then have to pull — coax was a better word — the spans closed again. It could take up to two hours to get across the river.

One time after school, Evelyn, Reg and Trev arrived at our Jervois Bridge berth only to find *home* was no longer there. After that, Father had an arrangement with the school principal to provide money for a taxi so that we children could make their way to wherever the *Inverlass* was moored. This could be several miles away, right the way to Outer Harbour, in fact. Father would reimburse him later.

## PORT ADELAIDE 1935 — THE FIRST SECRET

Our father Bert was fortunate, as an unskilled worker, to have employment at a time when one in every three men was out of a job. And he had had to chase the work too. He and Mum had done their best to make good on a 990-acre farm at the foot of Yorke Peninsula. Father purchased this land on reasonable terms as part of the Soldier Resettlement Scheme following his military service in the First World War. However, it was not good soil at the bottom of the peninsula. It was very rocky. Despite their efforts, it had been just too hard to clear enough land to get crops in the ground, bring them to harvest, sell what they managed to harvest at a reasonable price and, from that, pay our debt and make a living. Our parents had to leave the land and look for work on the peninsula and wherever else they could find employment.

Life on board the *Inverlass* was, depending on whose perspective you sought, either exciting and lots of fun, or plain hard work and compromise. My two brothers shared the first perspective, and my mother, the second. Evelyn did not seem to mind it too much, although she sorely missed her pony on the farm. I was small enough that the narrow confines of a ship did not bother me.

I think Mum really missed the space and freedom of life on the farm though. Take neighbours. On the farm even though neighbours might be some miles distant, they could be relied upon in times of need even when everyone was doing it tough. Farmers like Mum and Dad, starting out on their farms, did not have many cattle so when one of them could afford to kill a beast the neighbours would all share it. The next time it was another farmer who would kill a beast and we would all share again.

For general groceries, our parents would write out an order and post it off to town: that is, Adelaide which lay on the other side of Gulf St Vincent. This would happen every three months. The order would be packed in Adelaide at Reilly's and sent off by boat. A farmer would meet the boat at Edithburgh and bring down the groceries for a number of farmers in the area. The grocer would charge the account until the harvest cheque came in. Sometimes our order included a packet of sweets for the children — they were the most beautiful lollies a child ever had. Most of the time the family lived on homemade bread and jam. The jam used to come in seven-pound tins. The family also ate a lot of dripping (fat from the meat when it is cooked). I must add that I was not born then but heard these recollections from my older brother Reg.

Living on a ship in Port Adelaide, we were not all that far from neighbours in the surrounding suburbs but we were as cut off from them as if we, or they, were in another city. The sense of neighbourliness found in the country seemed harder to find in the city. In other ways, what neighbours we did have could be *too* close. Washing clothes was a trial on the hulks because of the neighbours. Not only did Mum have to watch the weather and note the wind direction, it was just as important to see what the boats nearby were doing. If they were coaling, well, it was not a washing day, lest grimy coal dust settle on newly washed clothes.

There were fewer coal hulks now as engines that ran on crude oil began to power commercial ships. Not counting ours, which didn't deal with coal anyway, there were two other coal hulks in the Port. The Roberts lived on one of these vessels, the *Marion*. Theirs was a sad situation. Mrs Roberts had died in childbirth while having her eighth child, who also died. Seven young children were left on this dilapidated old ship without a mother. The oldest daughter, herself only twelve years old, had to largely bear responsibility for the younger children while her father worked. The poor girl had to grow up and take on the worries of parenthood much more quickly than seemed fair. Like many others, this family benefitted from the charity and support of the Port Adelaide Methodist Mission.

Another hulk that was berthed beside ours for a period was the *Flinders* on which an older man called Christian lived alone. Ironically, given his name, Mr Christian used to get very drunk and come home singing and swearing as he staggered across our ship to get onto his. Mr Christian was an otherwise friendly old fellow and apparently spent quite a bit of time apologising to Mother each morning after his evening drinking.

Our living quarters were in the poop deck of the ship while the milling took place at the other end. During the day when the machinery was working, we had electricity in our quarters but not at night. Mother's daily chores included having to keep a sharp eye on me. When we first came aboard, I was just a baby and had a wooden box as a playpen. Later, when I was a toddler, it was more difficult for my parents. Steep ladders and the large hawser holes were a source of worry for them. Sometimes hatches had to be kept opened. Once when I was two years old, they tell me, I fell through a hatch, down a step to the 'tween deck'. I was lucky not to be hurt. Well, *that* would change.

Despite the number of onerous tasks in her day, Mum was not only an energetic person but someone who nurtured a positive outlook on life. She had a small box camera and used to take pictures of nearby vessels, observing the hubbub of a busy working port. Mum also kept some plants on board in small pots. She tended these with care and tenacity, as though they were the last vestiges of her life on the farm.

Father worked hard in this job too. Even a non-port-leaving vessel such as the *Inverlass* could provide Father with anxious nights when there were high tides and strong winds.

## PORT ADELAIDE 1935 — THE FIRST SECRET

One night the wind broke one of our mooring lines and Father had to rush another down quickly to avoid us going adrift. He used to be up and out of bed a lot on those nights.

It was probably the boys who most got to enjoy this wharf-bound ship life. They used to swim most days, in summer at least, and there was a small boat tied up to the wharf adjacent to our boat, from which they used to fish. Reg loved fishing and often supplied our mother with seafood to cook for the evening meal. On one of their local expeditions, Reg and Trev found an old canoe made of galvanized iron. They claimed it and planned to cruise around the river as captains of their own boat. Father saw it. As Trev could not swim, not properly anyway, Father cast their canoe into the bottom of the river to save at least one of them from being drowned.

Ships from overseas often tied up close to our ship. Some brought timber as cargo. At times, the wharf labourers were none too careful in their unloading and broke timber. Reg and Trev were allowed to collect and take these broken pieces back to the ship. This wood came in handy as we only had a wood stove for Mother to cook on.

These were hard times indeed for many people. South Australia had, by the mid 1920s, an economy that was really struggling even before the infamous stock market crash of 1929. Many of the copper mines had closed and the prices of wool, wheat and other commodities had flattened. There was less trade. The Port was no longer as busy as it had been and so unemployment rose. There was no dole. Those unemployed who had no other resources, like savings or well-off relatives, survived through a combination of government rations, local charity, and in some cases, petty crime. There was a joke that used to do the rounds. Q: What line of work are you in? A: Oh, we're in the iron and steel business. The joke was that the wife took in ironing while the husband would steal whatever he could to help the family survive.

Government agents used to hand out coupons and the impoverished could get a ration of meat, bread, sugar, tea and condensed milk. It was degrading to people's self-respect to be on the rations. We would, in due course, also come to a point where we needed the support of the local Methodist Mission to get by.

It was a volatile time. There were general strikes and there was civil unrest in the Port. In 1928, the Waterside Workers went on strike over changes to their industrial award. One stevedoring company decided to employ other people. These volunteer workers were marched to work under protection. But they were denounced as 'scabs'. Mobs would storm ships where they were working and beat them up. The extreme ill feeling between fellow Portonians, relating to whether they were union or non-union workers, lasted for many years.

In January 1931, there was a march of some 2,000 people from the Port to the city to protest over changes to the meat ration. The Government had decided that beef was too expensive and so the meat now supplied in exchange for ration coupons was generally a poor quality mutton. The marchers demanded beef. They got to Adelaide and were confronted by police lines. It wasn't clear whether it was the batons of the police or the placards of the demonstrators that became the first weapons used in the riot that ensued.

We weren't well-off living on a hulk but we were grateful that it provided us with a home and a living. The boys found that they had the best 'backyard' to explore and play in of any of the students in their school. Sometimes the expeditions brought harsh consequences. Reg climbed to the top of the mast which was approximately seventy feet above deck. He had been told not to do it as it was dangerous. But Reg wanted to see the view. He earned a lashing with a bit of rope — Father always seemed to know where it was when he wanted it. Reg's problem was that he would never give in by showing either tears or contrition, and so Father kept going. I can remember Mum bathing the lacerations on Reg's back. Trevor had an entirely different strategy to his older brother: he would cry out early on during any punishment and Father would let up.

After they left the farm, and before he and Mum settled in Port Adelaide, Father looked after a pig farm in the Hills. It belonged to a Mr Halliday who was a member of parliament in the early 1930s. There were about sixty pigs that had to be fed from waste vegetables from the market garden next to where we lived. We also had a cow for our use. Reg had to cut grass to feed her. This was a considerable imposition in Reg's mind, his view being, 'who wants to waste his time cutting grass for a cow?' Father's strap and Reg met a few more times over this. One day young Trev and Reg were playing in this same despised tall grass. Dad ordered grass cut for the cow, so Reg started cutting. Meanwhile, Trev hid in the grass. Reg found him, but unfortunately, it was with the point of his sickle sticking in his head. The result was much sympathy for Trev and more strap for Reg.

I wouldn't want to give the impression that Father was a cruel man. It was the discipline of the day — spare the rod and spoil the child. Reg had various clashes with those in authority, at least those with authority over him. He once referred to his primary school teacher, Mr Dansie, as a 'very strong man with the cane'. And even when he stayed with Aunty Josie and Uncle Wal (our father's brother), there were chores to be carried out and consequences for not doing them. Reg had to pump water from the well and carry it over to the chook yard, wash out all the dirt from their water tins and refill them. If he forgot, then Uncle Wal would provide a reminder by delivering a few cuts with the strap. But Reg never had a bad word to say against Uncle Wal. Like the rest of us, he was very fond of Uncle Wal. Instead, it was his duels with Aunty Josie that traumatised him. Aunty Josie had a thing about starting the day right. That meant that unless you said 'Good morning' to her, she would not allow you to have breakfast. Reg had a great hunger each morning, only matched, it seemed, by the size of his determination.

## PORT ADELAIDE 1935 — THE FIRST SECRET

The two of them, Aunty Josie and Reg, clashed something like this:

'Good morning, Reginald.'

'Hello, Auntie.'

No breakfast.

With greater feeling, 'Good morning, Reginald!'

'Hello, Auntie.'

Silence.

This stalemate would hold.

Finally, Reg would give in, 'Good morning, Auntie.'

'Good morning, Reginald.'

He could then eat. Having to submit like this went against the grain. Despite the many beatings he got as a boy, admittedly in part because of his steadfast determination to follow his own way, it was his disagreements with Aunty Josie, and not those beatings, that caused him to once remark, 'I still carry the scars.' He meant the scars in his mind and memory rather than the ones on his back. His motto was, 'Some of us don't like to be forced.' And yet Reg was someone, in Father's absence, who I came to rely on to look after me. He was like a father and helped me out all my life, even though he complained almost anytime he was asked to do anything! When I got married and asked him if he would give me away, he replied, 'Sure! I've been trying to do that for years anyway!'

My older sister Evelyn, by contrast, had a beautiful disposition. She always saw the best in people. I don't remember her speaking poorly of others and she was always ready for a chat, even with her little sister — I was eleven years younger than her. I don't know whether I was an afterthought or an accident as I came along six years after my brother Trevor who was next up from me. Evelyn used to sleep in a small room off the main saloon, and when I contracted chickenpox, she vacated it so that I could sleep in there away from everyone else. It was only to be for a few weeks, but the day I was cleared of the chicken pox, I came down with German Measles and had to spend another three weeks in Evelyn's bedroom. She didn't complain.

Evelyn loved to play basketball at school, and in the close confines of the galley, she often used to 'throw goals' with a loaf of bread, trying to get it in the bread tin. One time she tried it with a lettuce. That didn't please our mum.

By 1935, the economy was picking up and the grain milling on the *Inverlass* was no longer required. There was an increase in the tonnage and quality of the barley crop around the state and the market for grain was stronger. Our ship was sold by the Barley Board. It was suggested that the *Inverlass* be converted yet again, this time into a floating nautical museum for the State's Centenary celebration in 1936, but the proposition was rejected by the Port Adelaide Council. When the *Inverlass* was decommissioned, all the machinery on board was stripped off. To enable the machinery to be removed and sold, a number of holes were cut in the decks. Walking around on deck became quite hazardous. We lost two dogs as they fell through these holes to the bottom of the hold some 28 feet below. Both had to be destroyed because of their injuries. The older children, especially the two boys, would frolic on deck and jump over the holes. I was a kid, just six years of age, with short legs. One time, I was following my brothers in their antics, and I fell through a hole. Cries went out. They all thought I was dead. The fixed ladders into the hold had been removed so Father threw down a rope ladder and made the terrible climb down to retrieve me.

Father had a Hudson Essex and he whisked me off to the casualty hospital in Port Adelaide for preliminary first aid. From there, I was sent to the Children's Hospital. On the journey, I lay across my mother's lap wrapped in a grey blanket.

At hospital, they cut my clothes off with scissors and, following x-rays, I spent the next several weeks lying on my back, confined to bed. I had a fractured pelvis and spine as well as concussion and multiple bruises. Apparently, in my fall, I just missed hitting my head on two of the metal girders that braced the hull. It's sobering to consider how just a few centimetres can be the difference between a longevity of six years and one now exceeding ninety-three years.

I had to stop in hospital for over six weeks. Father left for Warooka on the Peninsula to the job that he had arranged earlier. This was working in W. Cadd's Grocery Store. Mum stayed in Adelaide with me and the other children. My accident changed the whole course of our lives. The plan had been that after leaving the *Inverlass*, we would all relocate to the Peninsula, but that didn't happen, it seemed, because of my accident. It was a confusing time for everyone. Father and Mother never got back together again. It was the end of the family as we had known it. For many years I blamed myself for this.

Near the end of my time in hospital, I was, with Mum's help, learning to walk again. To regain my walking, I had to build my unaided steps each day from one through to ten – adding just one extra step each day. When I could walk ten paces unaided, I was ready to be discharged. During my time in hospital, Mum and the children stayed with our Auntie Mavis, Mum's sister. When I came out of hospital, I was billeted for around three weeks with the Reverend Willason and his family in North Adelaide. Mum was busy trying to find accommodation for the five of us. We had known the Reverend Willason because he had been the minister at the Port Adelaide Central Mission. While I was there, Father came to visit me. When I saw him, I rushed across the room, jumped into his arms and he hugged me, with a twisting motion as you do when you want to make a hug last. This is an abiding memory in what was otherwise a blur. I don't recall anything else of what took place during his visit. He was soon gone.

## PORT ADELAIDE 1935 — THE FIRST SECRET

While I was at the Willason's, I accidentally broke a stirrup on a large and ornate wooden rocking horse. Even though I was small, I managed to turn the rocking horse around so that the side with the broken stirrup now faced the wall. Naturally, the first adult that entered the room asked, 'Why has the rocking horse been turned around?' I couldn't keep my mistake a secret.

And yet, it seemed that Mum and Dad were able to do that with theirs.

CHAPTER TWO

# Alberton 2015 — The First Conversation

I still love my football team. I am a member of the Port Adelaide Football Club Bequest Society. The club provides us with lunch and recognition a few times a year to say thanks to those of us who are supporting the club even after we pass on. Having had to stop driving my car, I now need a lift to these luncheons. Todd, from our church, first accompanied me in 2015 and has accompanied me a few times since. When I first invited him, I knew that he followed the footy and went to most games at Adelaide Oval. So, I thought he might be interested to come with me to the club at Alberton. He got a free lunch and an insider view for his trouble. On arrival, I would ride the old, snail-paced lift to the first floor with the other seniors. Because of its small capacity, there was no room for Todd. He would see me into the lift and then climb the stairs to meet me.

There might therefore have been a certain mutual benefit to our arrangement but we found each other's company to be very agreeable. It's funny because at church, usually at morning tea, we mostly confine our talk to discussing the fortunes of our footy team. But at the football club, we found ourselves talking about the community and our church.

The function room at the club is upstairs and overlooks the green turf of Alberton Oval. The expanse is like an oasis. And I think that with respect to the Port's industrial past, Alberton Oval was indeed an oasis for all of us. I told Todd at our first luncheon how William and I used to stand on the mound over there and watch home games. At half-time, we would walk home, back across the railway track, have a cup of tea, and return for the second half. It wasn't hard. It was that close. I was born nearby in Everton in 1929. The name has changed and it is now called Pennington.

I also told him about my first six years living on a ship moored in the inner harbour. I described how my father had been the caretaker of the coal hulk, the *Inverlass*, and how, in 1935 when it was decommissioned, Dad had lost his job.

Despite the noise of a packed luncheon room Todd was listening carefully and without interruption. I went on to relate the story of my fall into the hold, the subsequent breakup of our family, and how for many years I blamed myself for what had happened.

'Whoa, that's a heavy burden for a child to bear,' Todd responded. 'How did you cope with that? I mean, when did you come to see yourself as not being responsible for it?'

When *did* I come to not see myself as being responsible? It was a good question.

'Oh well, I suppose with the passing years I just came to terms with it. That would have been sometime in my mid-teens. I also learned, as I listened to the adults, that there was more to it than just my accident. There was talk of another woman.'

This was enough to produce a temporary silence. However, we moved on fairly easily to other matters. Todd was one of a small group that had started a community garden at the back of our church near the centre of the Port. I love this garden. So much so that, with my friends, I celebrated my 90th birthday in it. I asked Todd how things at the garden were going.

'It's going well, thanks, Ruth. The other day I had soil delivered to fill the new garden bed where Greentree stood.'

Greentree was a 1920s era building which had recently been pulled down. It had been a meeting hall and stood separate to the main church building. Sadly, it had become unsafe due to some structural issues, and it was going to cost too much to renovate. A newly constructed retaining wall now supported a raised garden bed — slightly under a half-tennis court-sized garden.

Todd continued, 'The driver, I can't remember his face, just his manner. He said, "I got seven tonnes of soil. Where do you want it?" I showed him and he dumped it via a hydraulically raised tipper. Then he got out of the cab, rubber mallet in hand, and smacked the underneath side of the inclined tray like a gong, one side and then the other, ferociously, as though he was angry at something. Soil that had resisted now slid meekly to the pile below. He climbed back into the cabin and directed me to secure the trailer flap with two pins once the tray was horizontal again. Only then, through the open cabin window, did he speak, "So ... community garden. Tell me about it." I explained, as concisely as I could — for it seemed words were not to be squandered — how we wanted to compost our waste and grow food organically to share with our local community. "Good," he responded. "The bloody boxes they're building these days," with a nod to recent housing developments in the Port. "No room for anything green or space to grow things. It's not healthy." By way of explanation, he added, "I'm into permaculture and all that shit." With that he drove off.

'I guess encouragement comes in different guises. But, what I like, Ruth, about the garden, apart from the beauty and the space, is the connection with our neighbours that it creates. We have a trolley upon which we put fresh produce from the garden, and we offer it to the passers-by. There are plenty of them. They go from Commercial Road through to Centrelink on Lipson Street. Some take things off the trolley, gratefully. Others ask, "What's going on here? Can we come in?" It feels neighbourly.'

Lunch at the club was always a two-hour event, presented informally but, nevertheless, structured carefully. There were welcome drinks, mains and dessert (each a choice of two options) spaced by interviews with an off-duty coach or player, and presentations of new members to the society. To bring things to a culmination there were the concluding raffles. It was well-sequenced and timed. The MC delivered well-worn jokes throughout. We all waited for them as if greeting old acquaintances. It was a bit of fun.

It started at midday, and by 2 pm, it was finished. However, on this first occasion, Todd and I had not noticed that the waiters had cleared the tables. Nor had it registered that the other guests had already mostly filed out. We had been engaged in intense and prolonged conversation.

When Todd picked me up for these Bequest Society lunches, he was generally on time. One time we arrived early at our table before anyone else. Each table setting had a name tag. Mine indicated a chair with its back to the stage. I said to Todd, 'I hate sitting with my back to the presentations. Do you think we could change the positions of the name tags?'

Todd deftly switched them and we sat down. The table began to fill with the other guests. One woman arrived and, upon seeing her position at the table, was not happy. 'I specifically asked to be facing the stage!'

## ALBERTON 2015 — THE FIRST CONVERSATION

There was the briefest catching of each other's eyes. I think it was the first indication that Todd and I could trust each other.

In 2020, COVID-19 put an end to the luncheons at the football club. Todd came to visit me at home instead. He had asked me whether he might find out more about my story. I was happy to do that. I enjoyed our conversations. Our meetings usually took place on a Thursday afternoon following my other commitments for the day. I had the gardener come in the morning and then the prayer group via Zoom at 11 am, followed by my Pilates class in Woodville shortly after lunch. Todd would come just after I arrived home around 2.30 pm.

Todd asked me about my early life and growing up. I told him about my parents and siblings; of my progress at school, work and church; and, of course, meeting William. I shared the lot really. I had no compunction about sharing such things. I think that I even surprised myself with what came out, warts and all. I suppose you get to an age where maintaining a certain persona is no longer that important.

Over the following eighteen months, his visits worked out to be about once every four to six weeks. Having asked for and received my consent to record our conversations, he would sit opposite me with a small recorder on his lap and an even smaller microphone, taped to a length of dowel, which he pointed in my direction.

They were congenial times. We discussed topics other than my life — such as the politics surrounding the use of the prison bar guernsey of our football team, how we handle scam callers on the phone, activities currently taking place in the community garden and, more seriously, questions hanging over the head of our congregation and church. Without setting a time, we would generally talk for an hour and a half, before sealing our conversation with a cup of Earl Grey tea and a piece of whatever cake I had in the kitchen at the time.

CHAPTER THREE

# Port Districts 1936-1954 — Making our Way

We moved to Alberton to a house that belonged to the mother of a family friend. Our backyard abutted her backyard. It wasn't a comfortable situation as we noticed that she used to stand, slightly crouched, at her back fence and listen to what was happening in our house. I suppose that Mum must have experienced new ways of feeling vulnerable now that Dad was gone — others standing by, and ready to criticise her.

Prior to my accident I had started primary school at Port Adelaide. Now I commenced at Alberton Primary. On my first day, I wouldn't let Mum pick me up from school because I didn't want people to think I was too young to go on my own — a funny notion given that I was only approaching seven years of age. On reflection, Reg was not the only headstrong child in the family. She took me to school and told me to come out of the gate at the end of classes and walk towards the trees. It was a gate that was facing the Port Road, the main thoroughfare connecting Port Adelaide and the city. The problem was that I came out of a different gate and walked towards the trees but in the wrong direction. The streets weren't familiar but then I was, myself, relatively new to Alberton. I kept walking, adhering to the directions I had been given but which I had misinterpreted, until I got to West Croydon. It was nearly dark. A hairdresser was just finishing work on a lady in her shop. She looked out and asked after me. Upon hearing my story, she said, 'Oh dear, you're at West Croydon. You're nowhere near Alberton'. I had walked almost five kilometres instead of seven hundred metres. She kindly offered to drive me home. On reaching Alberton, she had to spend more time helping me find our house in Queen Street because I wasn't sure what the number was.

Both Evelyn and Reg had, by now, left school and found work. Things had been quite hard for Mum before they were able to help with the household budget. Dad did send money but not regularly or reliably. We received firewood from the Mission for our cooking and heating. It was an initiative of the Reverend McCutcheon.

Reg's first job, which Father arranged, was with an undertaker, a chap named Deslandes. Father had wanted a bedroom suite made from timber that lined the captain's cabin on the *Inverlass*. Mr Deslandes and Reg had crafted a very serviceable bedroom suite (I have it in my house now some eighty-seven years later, and it has been offered to the Maritime Museum in Port Adelaide when I pass away) and after that job, Reg helped cut and plane timber for some of Mr Deslandes' coffins. Reg had to stop working there after my fall when he and Mum and the other children moved to Adelaide.

Reg was pretty good at finding work. It was not long before he started work at a café on commission. He would take lunch orders from around the various offices and deliver them on his bike at the time requested. For this he was paid a retainer of two shillings and sixpence per week. Plus, he received two shillings in every twenty he collected, a ten percent commission. Totalled for the week, this was good money for a fifteen-year-old. His boss seemed to realise this and said to Reg that he was tired of working out his wages every week and offered him a set wage of twelve shillings and sixpence per week. It was half of what he had been earning. Reg quit. He found work at the Flinders Tractor Co. This lasted eighteen months before he was laid off because the demand for second-hand parts for tractors had fallen away.

At one point, Reg and Trev procured a contract to clear all the pigeons from the eaves and roof spaces of the Port Adelaide Railway Station and some other buildings in the Port. They had become a pest – the pigeons, not the boys. The accumulation of pigeon poo put extra weight on structures and blocked vents and drains. The boys would go out at night, climbing up to the tops of the buildings where they trapped the pigeons and later sold them to a delicatessen. Mum was always frightened that they might fall. They didn't, and both went on to apprenticeships.

Reg became a first-class turner. He worked for the company APAC Industries from 1936 until 1984 when he retired. He started by putting pinions on car jack bodies. On his first day, Reg had to pick up a pinion and fit a pin into it, and then hammer it into a jack body. This was supposed to be done 105 times an hour. There were thousands to be done. As soon as he finished a heap of completed pinions, they were removed by someone with a wheelbarrow. The same person kept bringing more to do. The best Reg could do on his first day was 90 parts per hour. His foreman warned him that he had to do better on his second day or he would be fired. On the second day he made 100 per hour. The same warning was given. By the third day he made the required 105 average. Work conditions were strict. Smoking was only allowed for ten minutes at 10 o'clock and 2 o'clock but nobody was allowed to stop work or waste time making cigarettes to smoke. If you did not make them before work, you were not allowed to waste time doing so there.

Every boy, as he got older, was afraid that he would be fired because when they turned twenty-one, these boys had to be paid full money — a man's wages. Reg was lucky in one way because by the time he turned twenty-one, he was a first-class turner and working in the gun annexe making anti-tank gun parts. The war had started in 1939 and the company was co-opted for munitions work. Reg did not serve in the Armed Forces as he was in an industry considered to be vital for the war effort. He did enrol in the Alberton branch of the Volunteer Defence Corps which was an Australian part-time volunteer military force modelled on the World War II British Home Guard.

Trev was good at woodwork and gained a credit in the subject at school. In 1938, he was apprenticed as a carpenter at Grove & Son and went on to gain a first-class pass in carpentry and joinery at trade school. During the war years, Trev served in the Air Force. He was discharged after the war in 1946, the same year he got married, with the rank of Leading Aircraftman. This was a trades-related rank. He was an air mechanic. Trev would become a Clerk of Works for several construction companies and later site foreman for a local construction company, Fricker and Co. Trev did a lot of travelling with his work — all over the state. Perhaps it was this that contributed to some of his future sadnesses.

Evelyn started working at Coles serving behind the counter. The Reverend McCutcheon's daughter worked at Coles and I think she got her a job. At school, Evelyn had excelled. She went to a technical college. I greatly admired Evelyn's skill with her hands. Her needlework was superb. She tried to teach me tatting but my fingers were not nimble enough. My skill was rather with paper and design. Evelyn was very clever and won seven blue ribbons in one year.

You had to be dux in each subject to get a blue ribbon. She topped every course that she did. Later, she burnt them. Oh, I could never get over that! I would never have done that.

She also played piano, and did so very well. She played at the Sunday school anniversaries. Often there were over a hundred singers in the choir and many more watching on in the congregation. At one of these anniversaries, Evelyn performed the very hard-to-play, 'The Holy City'. I was so proud of her.

Evelyn moved on to work as a milliner at a company called G&R Wills in Adelaide. This is what she had hoped to do. They used to get hats to trim. She became unwell and was diagnosed with tuberculosis. The doctor surmised that she had probably picked up the *tubercle bacillus* from one of the hats that had been brought in for millinery work. She had to have gold injections and couldn't work for five years. She was about eighteen when she first contracted TB and had to have a bedroom on her own. We used to go to the Hills every year on medical advice, so that we could be out of the dust and the heat of the city. Mum rented a little cottage in Stirling that was part of a property owned by the Morton family. She rented it each summer for four or five years. When we were at the Port in the winter, and she was still housebound, Evelyn would watch me go off to school with my case, later telling me, 'I'd stand at that window and

I'd think, *Oh, that poor little thing with those little legs, having to walk all the way to school.*'

I loved my older sister dearly, but there were some habits of hers that really annoyed me. Cutting slices of bread or cake, for instance. Evelyn didn't mind how she cut a slice from a loaf of bread or a piece of cake. She would just sort of hack it off in either case without much care, whereas I always felt that the slices needed to be cut straight and evenly. We locked horns not a few times over that. Funny that we would have such differences in outlook.

After the eavesdropping landlady of Alberton, we were glad of the opportunity to move to Semaphore. It was a church contact that enabled this. Mrs Bridge, a lady from church, had a brother, a Mr Cunningham, who owned a fruit shop at Semaphore. He needed a housekeeper. We went there and Mum looked after the house and cooked for him. Reg also used to help Mr Cunningham with some of his chores. We lived upstairs behind the fruit shop. Mr Cunningham was a terrific fellow and used to supply us with fruit and veg from his shop.

I was eight years old when we were living at Semaphore. On Anzac Day that year, everyone went to the march. I was out the back by myself, sitting on the seat. I must have said that I wasn't feeling well or something. Afterwards, Mum came out and asked me what was wrong. I said, 'I'm just sad that I didn't go to the march.' I know that sounds circular: I didn't go to the march because I wasn't feeling well, and yet here I was, putting my malaise down to *not* going to the march. The fact was that all the other kids at school had fathers who were marching. I didn't have my father. He was living in the country. It saddened me because, at that stage, I still felt like his absence was my fault. Father sent us birthday cards every year and the occasional gift.

Mum insisted that all the family should go to Semaphore beach for the January 28$^{th}$ holiday. It was a great production and took ages to pack for. We would then catch the train, traipse down to the beach, put up a shade, spend the day getting sunburnt, and come home full of sand in everything. We repeated this every year for several years.

We often went over to the Peninsula to stay on Grandfather's farm at Corny Point. They were Dad's parents, although, Gran wasn't Dad's natural mother. She had died of heatstroke when Dad and his two brothers, Wal and Harry, were small children. Grandfather Fewster had married again. I didn't ever meet Mum's mother. She also died before we were very old. I met Mum's dad once, not long before he died. He was sitting up in bed, a wizened scrap of a man with an untrimmed beard. In contrast, I knew my other grandfather well. Grandfather Fewster was a tall rangy fellow. Once, he had an emergency appendix operation, and three days later, he was back up on his horse. I was absolutely astounded by that and have always remembered it. How could he do it? Grandfather Fewster was indeed a raw-boned Aussie bloke. He had worked hard, using his body, all his life. He and Gran were wheat farmers. They also had cows and were reasonably self-sufficient with milk, cream and butter. They used to sell cream.

Grandfather and Gran just accepted us, even though Dad was not there with us. Gran was a sweetie. She didn't talk much but if she said something everyone listened. Mum was well accepted as daughter-in-law. We all were. We'd all turn up and Gran would find beds for us. It was a happy experience except for the time Mum and I were staying over, and Grandfather 'bailed us up' in bed one morning. What I mean by that is, Grandad came in to say good morning and, on this occasion, sat on the end of the bed and proceeded to extol the truth of Seventh Day Adventism. Since Mum and I were in bed and he was sitting on the end of the bed, we couldn't get up. We had to wait until he ran out of steam. He tried to convert us a few times. Nonetheless, Grandfather Fewster was kind, very kind.

Trev and Reg must have stayed home on one of our visits to the Peninsula. Possibly Reg had to go to work. They also used to love visiting Grandfather and Gran at Corny Point and to have the opportunity to work alongside their uncles on the farm. In our absence, Trev and Reg were playing cards one evening at home in Semaphore when a mouse came out from under a cupboard. They decided to set a trap and catch it. As fast as they could set the trap they caught a mouse. There were thirteen in all before the action ceased. In a less harsh but no less real eviction, Mr Cunningham, our landlord, married his mate's widow and so, after a relatively short time living in Semaphore, we were on the move once more.

Mum found a place on Commercial Road, the main road into Port Adelaide. The Mission may have helped her find it — I'm not sure. We lived above and behind a tailor's shop. The tailor was on the corner, a hairdresser was next door to him and there was a bootmaker next to the hairdresser. We became friends with all of them. It was opposite the Congregational church where I go now some eighty years later, even though we did not attend church there at that time. Our church, the Methodist church, was just around the corner in Dale Street.

We were next to the large produce markets. Living above the shop, we had a balcony, and I used to be up on the balcony on Friday evenings. People would walk underneath us on their way to the market. It was open at other times but Friday night was the big night for the market. Everybody went. The entrance was where the KFC is now. It was a big iron shed. I wasn't allowed to go because I was too young and might get into trouble. I had to watch everybody else go. They sometimes brought me back pieces of watermelon. The market was more than fruit and veg though. There were all sorts of things. Going to the market on Friday nights was an outing that people looked forward to.

I was reasonable at school without rising to Evelyn's heights. I went for three years to Woodville High. In those days you got your QC (Qualifying Certificate) and then you went on to the Leaving Certificate. The day came for me to sit for my QC but I got appendicitis. They operated on me, removing my appendix, on the day of the main exam. So, I missed this all-important event. Mr Biddle was the teacher. He gave me a report that said I had done the work and reached the required standard but that, through unfortunate circumstances, I wasn't able to sit the exam. So, I got my QC that way. They didn't have supplementary exams in those days. Everyone said that I was 'Mr Biddle's pet'. This was the continuance of a theme: my siblings all thought I was spoiled. The boys always said I was the pet and could do no wrong. It never seemed that way to me. However, I can never remember Mum hitting me. She never raised her hand to me at all. I must have made her cross sometimes.

I became a member of the Wesleyan Methodist Church in Port Adelaide at the age of twelve. I had been going to Sunday school since I was four. Now I was teaching Sunday school, not long after my twelfth birthday. Everyone, apart from my brothers, said I was very solemn and very grown up. I also joined the Methodist Girls' Comradeship. The Comrades, as it was known, was a training ground for young women. It encouraged social, physical and educational development. It had a strong devotional aspect too — learning to put Christian faith into practice. You weren't supposed to go into Comrades until you were fifteen years old, but they let me in three years early because they thought I was mature. Evelyn was already in Comrades and so having a sister there helped me find my way.

Even at this age, I had a certain gravitas, and Mum seemed to come to me for advice. To my knowledge, she didn't go to Evelyn in this same way. She wouldn't do anything, wouldn't make a decision, without asking my opinion or checking it out with me. Mum said later that I was sillier at twenty-three than I was at twelve. 'When you were twelve you were a serious child and you made serious decisions,' she said. Mum blamed William, who was courting me when I was in my early twenties, for that. He made a joke out of almost everything. I think my serious demeanour arose from the fact that Father had left, and I always felt responsible for Mum. I felt that I had to look after Mum.

While we were living at Commercial Road, Evelyn turned twenty-one. We had fish for tea which was something special as we were quite poor. Mum made a cake. I remember being wrapped up in a rug on the chair near the fire as I was not very well. I found it difficult to swallow the fish. We all sang 'Happy Birthday,' and Evelyn cut the cake. They had to get the doctor to me next morning, and he looked down my throat and said, 'I am sorry but you have diphtheria.' This was quite a serious disease and had been known to block the sufferer's windpipe leading to suffocation. I spent the next eight weeks in Northfield Infectious Diseases Hospital.

This was an age when everyone, not just the poor, was amenable to various serious illnesses. After Evelyn got sick with TB, the whole family, minus Dad, spent the ensuing summers up in the cottage in Stirling. Reg used to travel up and down to Stirling by motorbike. Trev, who was also working, came with Reg on the back. It was a little two-stroke. They used to arrive up there quite late after work, and they did this for the duration of our stay, which would be several months.

The cottage in Stirling was like our second home. Put this way, it sounds misleading as we didn't even own a first home. Putting that aside, at Stirling, Mum and I shared one bedroom, and the boys shared the other. Evelyn slept on the verandah for the fresh air. There was a kitchen but no refrigerator. Few people had them. We had a cool safe. It worked a bit like evaporative air conditioning. Water dripped through hessian that hung around the sides of the safe. The safe itself was like a mesh-sided cupboard. Air passing through the wet hessian then kept the foodstuffs inside the safe cool. We also used to fill bottles with water, tie a long string on the neck, and lower them into the Mortons' well to get them cold.

Each night Mum would place a glass of milk and a piece of fruit on a small table alongside Evelyn's bed out on the veranda. One night a possum discovered the fruit. The cottage had a big fig tree beside it. It might have come down from that. Evelyn slept through the experience but was quite unnerved the next morning on finding out about her night visitor. After that the fruit always had to be put in a container.

We saw quite a lot of the Morton family. We became good friends. They had a daughter Beryl who was my age. They also had a son who was about our Trev's age. Mrs Morton was a small lady. She had lost her sense of taste and smell. We never really found out the reason for this but it must have been most uncomfortable for her. With Mrs Morton, everything had to be done correctly, and we did our best to comply.

One summer there were bushfires which were very bad. The heat was excessive. The fires started to creep closer to the hill on which the Mortons' house and cottage was situated, so Mum sent Evelyn and me to the general store. I guess that she was staying to help defend the property. The store was some distance from the fires and in a large clearing and was a refuge. I wouldn't go without my celluloid baby doll, so Mum told me I could take it, but if the fire came too close, I had to throw it away. Holding Evelyn's hand with one hand and clutching the doll with the other, I walked down the road to the store, bawling my eyes out because I might have to throw my doll away. We stayed there a long time and then went home. I don't remember Evelyn giving any hint that she was scared but I know I was.

I suppose our only other regular escape from the Port was in visiting Grandfather and Gran Fewster on the Peninsula. Gran was a wonderful cook. One day in the kitchen Gran was baking, and Evelyn picked up what she thought was a raisin from the table only to discover, after she put it in her mouth, that it was a bee. Great spluttering followed.

That reminds me of an occasion when it was me who would do the spluttering. I was about nine. Evelyn and Al, Evelyn's boyfriend who would later marry her, took me to see a film, *Rainbow on the River*, with Bobby Breen. It was in the Alberton Odeon Picture Theatre. The building is still there and is at the bottom of the street where I live now. It has long since become a small shopping centre. In the 1930s, Bobby Breen was a child star whose fame was on a par with that of Shirley Temple. He had an angelic voice and used it to tug at everyone's heartstrings. I remember being terribly excited when Evelyn and Al invited me to go with them, as going to the pictures was a very rare treat. In *Rainbow on the River*, Bobby Breen played a young boy, Phillip, who was an orphan of the US Civil War. Phillip had been lovingly raised by a former slave, Toinette. At great sacrifice, she saved her money and planned to send her beloved young 'son' to school. However, a priest found out about some distant relatives of Phillip, and the boy was uprooted from his happy existence with Toinette and sent to live far away, where he was treated badly.

Whenever I am watching anything, even now, I am right there and feel part of the action. Well, when Bobby faced his hardships, I became so distraught I cried and cried. Unfortunately, not quietly. I sobbed my way through the whole of the film even though it ended happily for Bobby's character, Phillip. Al declared that he would never take me to another film as long as he lived. And he didn't. He never let me forget it.

Al had to work quite hard to show his bona fides to Mum as a prospective son-in-law. I remember a picnic we had in the Hills. It was a wet day but we decided to go anyway. We caught the train to the city and then another to the Hills, getting off at Belair. Mum and Evelyn had made a batch of cream puffs that were packed in a case which Al carried 'on the flat' so they wouldn't squash. Poor fellow, he was like a butler carrying some precious family heirloom. We found a little shelter shed and huddled there in the rain. We couldn't get out to enjoy the Hills, and the only bright spot in the day was eating the cream puffs. At last, it was time to come home again on the train.

Evelyn married Al when I was twelve. It was 1941 and Evelyn was twenty-three. Father came down from the Peninsula and gave Evelyn away. I was a *miniature* bridesmaid for the wedding. I appropriated that title as I was the only one not to have a partner. I was deemed too young for that.

Our aunts and uncles came down from the country too. I am not sure how Mum felt at the time, but afterwards, my brothers and I went with Dad and two of the uncles to the trots at Wayville Showgrounds. We had a great time with them. I had never been to the trots, but here was I, feeling grown up and going to the trots with my father.

Both our parents had been expert horse riders on the farm. The Fewsters loved horses. Dad's younger brother Harry loved nothing more than to break in unsaddled or wild horses. They would throw themselves backwards to try and unseat him, but Uncle would jump out of the saddle and wait for them to stand up again. He would then leap onto their back once more and continue riding. Once, during a rodeo at the Wayville Showgrounds, Uncle Harry harnessed three horses to a wooden board and, standing on this board, drove those horses at full gallop around the arena. He said later that the board made a good mock chariot. He was a bit of a daredevil, our Uncle Harry.

I did not see Dad again for another seven years after Evelyn's wedding. Our next meeting would prove to be a disaster.

## CHAPTER FOUR

# Retreat to the Garden

In the time of my childhood, Port Adelaide was still very much a working port. The inner harbour was also known locally as the Port River, even though it was really an estuary and not really a river. The Port River was a busy place with a multiplicity of barques, ketches, tugs and ferries competing for passage to get to or from their moorings. There was ceaseless movement of people and cargo. Visiting seamen from around the world arrived with their own needs, namely, society and companionship, and these created a strong market in the Port for the provision of alcohol and sex.

In 1866, the Congregationalists bought a large block of land along Commercial Road from the Port Land Company, after the church they had built on the corner of St Vincent Street and Lipson Street burnt down. The new building on Commercial Road was erected quite quickly for its size. It was constructed in a neo-Gothic style using local sandstone from Dry Creek. Newspapers carried reports of 2,600 people attending services on the day of the building's opening in 1868.

There had been a longstanding tug-of-war between the various Christian churches in the Port and its many hotels, numbering around fifty, for the loyalty and patronage of the residents. This tension had reached its climax some fifteen years before the Fewster family moved onto the *Inverlass*. The forces of piety, led by Congregationalist minister, the Reverend JC Kirby, were victorious in getting legislation passed to force hotels to close at 6 pm. Those advocating sobriety did not just do so from a moralistic position. They did so with the idea of improving the social conditions for many Port Adelaide women and their families, as it was they who bore the brunt of alcohol abuse.

The Congregational church on Commercial Road remains a handsome, imposing building — a cathedral for the working class of the nineteenth century, you might say. It stood monumentally. If you were out the back looking at it, as Todd regularly did while working in the garden, the morning sun caused pleasing variations of colour and texture on the stonework. The building had an elegance that had not diminished in over 150 years. It made a statement that spoke permanence. But this only betrayed the extent of change swirling in and around it.

Todd has never been what was called, in the old-time parlance, a 'churchman'. He recalled his own coming to the Port Church in late 1979. Geoff, the minister at the time, had invited Todd to live with some other young adults in a community house at Largs Bay on the Peninsula. Eva had been one of them. One side of the house was residential while the other side was non-residential and could be used as a craft, music or meeting space. Local youth would come and spend time there.

Todd did not attend Sunday morning worship services at the Port Church. He went to a Sunday evening 'house church'. Sensing Todd's ambivalence about Sunday morning worship, Geoff had said about the house church, 'That's church. You don't need to also come to worship on Sunday morning.'

The community had been an exciting place to live in. Sometimes, going to work seemed, for Todd, like having a rest from the drama and energy of community life. There was unpredictability. Things were stolen or people turned up late at night looking for somewhere to sleep. But it was authentic and welcoming, and friendships were made.

One of these was between Todd and Eva. They fell in love. Just over a year following their wedding, they went to Afghanistan and worked there for four years. Todd was a physiotherapist and Eva, a nurse/midwife. For them, this was an extension of what they had been doing in the Port. That is, spending time with those on the periphery. In Afghanistan, this translated to helping improve access for many people who had little or no chance of health care and rehabilitation.

All in all, and over a long period, Todd had been able to skirt his uneasy relationship with the institutional church, mostly by not spending too much time in it.

In 2016, a group of over-35's at the Port Church asked the congregation for permission to start a worship service offsite — like a house church. Unfortunately, it did not meet with a favourable response. The older members of the congregation expressed the idea that another worship service, off-site, would fragment the congregation at a time when numbers were dwindling and folk needed to stick together. In retrospect, someone should have told the 35ers (as they were known) that there was a time-honoured 'tradition' at Port Adelaide where members who had an idea for a ministry just went ahead with it and recruited interest and support along the way. Geoff used to say, 'It's easier to ask for forgiveness than it is permission.'

The group left the church. They were around five or six families with young children. It was traumatic for the remaining members of the congregation. Synod sent a team (at the congregation's request) to interview everyone to try to understand what had taken place. In their final report, the departure was expressed as the spreading of wings: these young people needed to go out and find new horizons.

Todd was troubled by the findings of this review. The underlying reasons for the 35ers leaving had been largely ignored. This report did the congregation no favours. They had wanted change and perceived that there would be ongoing resistance to it. If the congregation could not face this then it did not augur well for dealing with the harsh, existential realities that lay ahead.

Todd felt bad on other counts. He had not supported the younger leadership as he should have. However, things were never that simple. It seemed that part of the change the group wanted was a more conservative expression of the gospel, something he had discerned through various conversations. It had been some years since the church had employed a minister. The financial resources were not available for that. The church ran via a ministry of the laity. Different members took turns in fulfilling different functions. Todd was on the preaching roster.

Living in a war zone in Afghanistan had brought Todd and Eva into distressing contact with suffering. The suffering was relentless and came in waves, buffeting and destroying people's lives. In witnessing these things at close hand, Todd and Eva had not been unaffected. These experiences had caused them to rethink previously held assertions commonly professed in biblical doctrine. The old explanations regarding why God apparently 'blessed' some and not others, or conversely, why some people suffered so much more than others, had worn untenably thin for them.

Todd was a university lecturer. He was practised in the structure and delivery of messages to young adults. Being an academic, he had also been trained in how to interpret texts (scriptural or otherwise). It did not appear to be a deficit in either of these skills which prompted the feedback he received from various of the 35ers. In what was something of a summary statement for her peers, one young woman had told him that she liked her sermons, 'old fashioned'.

Todd once preached on the story of Jesus asleep in the boat on the Sea of Galilee. An intense squall had enveloped the boat and those in it. The disciples were terrified. Jesus, however, continued to sleep. The disciples had cried out, 'Teacher, don't you care if we drown?'

Todd suggested to the congregation that none of us was quarantined from times where we might find ourselves alone and desolate, and where God, it seemed, was like Jesus in this story, 'asleep in the boat'. What could we make of this? Essentially, it was an invitation to consider how interventionist we could expect God to be in our lives: could we face tragedy and loss as part of the human condition without always expecting rescue? He was approached afterwards with the words, 'I wonder whether you even love God.' This shocked him. To his credit, the person rang Todd a couple of days later and apologised. It was a generous gesture but did not discount what had caused his reaction in the first place.

On another occasion, he preached on 'guilt' by drawing on contemporary neurophysiological understandings of pain. As an academic physiotherapist with a PhD, he was familiar with this research. The gist of it was that acute pain has an important protective and regulative function in the body — it awakens us to any threat of damage to body tissues, from whatever source. In contrast, chronic pain (carcinogenic pain being an exception) is an output via neural pathways from various centres in the brain, which redefines 'threat' in multiple and unhelpful ways. The result of this neural activity is that the patient experiences real pain but that this pain is modulated — turned 'up' or 'down' — by the person's perceptions of events and personal experience. Importantly, this pain, unlike acute pain, is not necessarily a consequence of actual damage to body tissues.

Todd compared this to guilt, suggesting that 'acute guilt', like acute pain, was a necessity that awakened our consciences to situations which needed our attention — not unlike damage to our moral integrity. Such situations might include the thoughtless or intended use of words or actions towards others or our complicity or apathy in situations of greater injustice. On the other hand, 'chronic guilt', whilst real, was like chronic pain. It had little or no actual function. It was more a learned and habitual response to situations in life and was needlessly disabling. Chronic guilt may require attention but for different reasons to the guilt associated with a healthy and functioning conscience.

Again, one of the 35ers came up to him afterwards and said, 'But Todd, I have no guilt.' It was a response that seemed to be based in Romans 8:1, 'There is therefore now no condemnation for those who are in Jesus Christ.' It was another piece of commentary on Todd's theology. And Todd could not deny the quiet loosening of the hold of doctrinal orthodoxy on his and Eva's thinking — not in one fell swoop but over time and in the context of their life experiences.

It was not that Todd explicitly expressed the changes in his theology in his sermons — he would not want to impose that. However, he did believe that expressing biblical stories and texts through the lens of acquired life experience, much of which was harsh and confronting, might paradoxically encourage others. But this was not the case. The most insightful and useful comment that Todd received came at a birthday party for one of the toddlers of the 35ers. John had said, 'Todd, we respect you and Eva and the others, but we just don't see a way of following where you are going.' It was a penetrating observation and one that was well-made.

It was as if the 35ers were looking at him, and perhaps others in the congregation, as Christians who had a washed-out and pale theology that was hard to identify, let alone follow. The 35ers didn't feel, with justification, as though the rest of the congregation was open to change. And yet, it was Todd who had changed too much.

The problem, on one level, might be described in terms of a clash between progressive and conservative theology. But, for Todd, it was not simply that. After all, Todd and Eva had been much more conservative in their views when they were the same age. His regret was more about the lost opportunity for these different age groups, spanning two generations, to encourage each other in navigating the rips and breaks of life, than it was to promote particular theological views.

The flip side of their leaving was a loss of confidence for Todd in being able to articulate what it was he now believed, not so much personal values — he was still clear on that — but as a Christian. It was a galling question for a teacher: had he nothing of worth to pass on? It was also like the rule in making ginger beer: ensure that you keep enough of the old batch in order to start the new one. He was not sure that he had. The old symbols, language and patterns of church life spoke to him less and less. The fizz had gone.

Todd decided to discontinue preaching in the church. As it turned out, he was not the only one who felt like leaving the church. But he could not bring himself to do that yet. There were longstanding friendships and his relationship with Eva to consider. And there was certainly no other church that he could see himself attending. As an interim decision, Todd decided to retreat to the community garden at the back of the church. It now had a name, The Bent Pine. The name described how he felt about faith and church – weathered and on a precarious lean.

CHAPTER FIVE

# Port Adelaide 1945-1960 — Working and Waiting

After graduating from Woodville High, I looked for work. I was sixteen. It was January 1945 and World War II would end later that year in November. We went to a friend of Dad's to see if he would take me on in his business. It was a transport company. He said that he didn't have any positions but the only place he would suggest that a young girl go to work in transport would be to Port Carriers with Mr Good. I went there and presented myself at their office and asked if they had any positions. A Mr Fraser, who was the company secretary, said that he didn't know and that he would have to speak with Mr Good. Mr Good was the Mayor of Port Adelaide and an elder in the Congregational church as well as being the owner of Port Carriers. I received a letter a couple of days later asking me to come for an interview. Following my interview with Mr Good, I was taken on. He said, 'I'm supposed to give you twenty-five shillings but I'll start you on thirty shillings per week.' I commenced with Port Carriers as a message girl. I quickly went from message girl to telephonist.

Our customers used to ring through their orders and, as the telephonist, I used to record them in a book and then tell the people in the store what we needed. They would load the ordered goods on trucks and take them to the city to deliver to the stores on their run. The first entry I ever made was a bill of loading and it was to pick up some goods from the ship, *Era*. It was four bales of 'duck' which was heavy canvas material. It had been ordered by Murdoch's, a company that made awnings and blinds. They were in the city: *Murdoch's awnings and sun blinds ... offer unlimited possibilities for the artistic protection and enhanced beauty of your home* ran their advertisement in the *Advertiser*. I've still got the page with that first ever entry. When I left the company all those years later, I asked if I could have it, and I tore the page out of the book.

Murdoch's was where William, my future husband, worked, and our introduction occurred via the telephone calls I made and received between Port Carriers and Murdoch's. Apparently, he liked the sound of my voice. He also said — not at that time, of course — that the cracked skull I sustained in my fall when I was six explained who I was. He was irreverent and always joking. He never failed to get a rise out of my mother. Perhaps he was the counterpoint for my gravitas, and it was this that kept me interested through some very challenging periods in our long courtship.

When I started work with Port Carriers, the company still had a horse and dray to carry goods for them. There were a lot of horses in the Port at that time. Most of the transport companies still had horses and drays. Then Port Carriers purchased a little old Ford truck. It was one of the smallest trucks, not much different in size to an ordinary ute today. The trucks gradually got bigger as time went on. Years later, the original Port Carriers truck, with the sign still on it, was found on a farm in the mid-north. Someone came across it rusting in a paddock and sent me a photo. As the business grew, the trucks became bigger and bigger until they were using prime movers with massive trailers that they could take off and put on.

Our transport route was from the Port Docks to the city and back. Our company in Divett Street, Port Adelaide, had three levels: a cellar and two storeys. We stored a lot of cartons of tinned products for Imperial Canned Foods. Murdoch's was also the agent for Imperial. One of their popular products was tinned lamb and sheep tongues. We also carted asbestos for James Hardie. I suppose nowadays each product would be regarded as unpalatable for different reasons.

I loved my job at Port Carriers. I worked there for twenty-seven years. Mr Good treated me like a daughter. He came to regard me as a replacement for his daughter who had died in childbirth. He said that to me more than once.

Oh, he was wonderful! Before he retired, he gave me some shares in the business, saying, 'They're not worth much now but down the track they may be worth something.' It didn't please his family. Sometime later, Mr Good's nephews, who then ran the transport side of the company, badgered me to give them back, arguing that the business was no longer thriving and that the shares still weren't worth anything to me. I did so. In one way they were right, they ran the company with less aplomb and less success than Mr Good, and the shares weren't worth what Mr Good had envisaged. You have to choose which battles to fight, and this one wasn't that important. Whenever I found myself in difficult situations and got upset, William always reminded me that I did not have to win every battle in order to win the war.

It would have been early in 1948, around the time of my nineteenth birthday, that my mother went to the country for a holiday with Gran and Grandfather. She left me a birthday present. It was a jug and six glasses. I must have had to stay in town and work. When I was younger I always went with her, but when I attended high school, there were times that I did not accompany Mum and, instead, stayed with Evelyn and Al in their sleepout.

One time when I was fifteen, I was staying with Evelyn and Al when we had a call from the hospital for me to go in to have a lump removed from my nose. Evelyn was concerned that as I had to be in there early in the morning and was to be operated on that day, I wouldn't have any food for a long time. She prepared me a good breakfast so I wouldn't get hungry. We obviously hadn't read the instructions very well because when the nurse asked me if I had eaten that morning, I said, 'Yes.' She then asked me what I had eaten. I replied, 'A chop and an egg.' Her response was to repeat what I had said, but with higher volume and a tone of incredulity, '*A chop and an egg?*' Her composure returned and a more familiar nursing voice opined, 'Well, you can't have an anaesthetic then.' She informed the doctor and they decided to give me a needle in my hand and not a mask over my face. As it turned out, Evelyn did me a favour since I had been dreading the mask over my face and the dripping of ether. The needle in my hand was a doddle.

What I want to tell you now, though, was most definitely not a doddle.

I'd a feeling that Mum had let me know, around the time of my nineteenth birthday, that Dad wanted to come and visit me. I was at home at our place in Commercial Road by myself. Reg and Trev had both married by then and lived away. Dad may have also written to me. He always sent me birthday cards. Anyway, he contacted me somehow and asked if he could come and have a meal with me. Well, as a nineteen-year-old, I was not used to cooking meals for anyone. Not guests, anyway. He came and it was the most uncomfortable meal I ever had in my whole life. Neither of us knew what to talk about. We had nothing in common. It was just so hard. The previous occasion on which we had seen each other, Evelyn's wedding, was not a time to build a relationship. And now, some seven years later, and thirteen in total since he walked out on us, he was trying to talk to me like a father. I just couldn't cope with that. It was a short stay. I don't even know what we talked about. We had our meal together and he disappeared. There was just no connection because we hadn't seen each other. He was trying to build a connection, I know, but I couldn't do it.

Reg courted Gwen in the shadow of war. Petrol ration tickets were needed to obtain petrol. He was allowed two gallons (about nine litres) every month. This allowed him to drive to Enfield from Port Adelaide to take Gwen to the pictures in Adelaide on a Saturday night and make the return journey. The rest of the month, the car had to stay at home. He rode a push bike out to see her. It was eight miles (thirteen kilometres) each way. On most Sunday afternoons, they would walk to Adelaide and return. That simple pleasure was loved. Occasionally, Reg would take Gwen and her family out to Tea Tree Gully to see her grandmother, spending the day there.

Gwen was working with her sister in a clothing factory machining industrial equipment — leather gloves, aprons, kitbags and general safety equipment. Reg would go to town when he was on afternoon shifts and meet her for lunch. It was the only way that he could see her during the week.

They married in 1944. The Reverend McCutcheon did the officiating. Afterwards they caught the bus to Mount Gambier for their honeymoon. Reg and Gwen had both lived through the Great Depression and the austerity and shortages imposed by World War II. This would lead Reg to build his own house, over several years, with the help of friends, including brother-in-law Al and brother Trev. While Reg and Gwen's house slowly took shape, they lived in another self-built 'granny flat' at the back of their block.

It took them six months to build this granny flat to the stage where they could move in. It was the middle of winter and they hadn't enough money to buy ceiling sheets. It was cold at night so they would pile clothes on the bed to try to keep warm and, by extension, healthy. When they first moved into the granny flat, the laundry, toilet and bathroom weren't finished so they used a telephone box and a bucket. This set-up was hidden in a clump of bamboo bushes that was growing in the corner of the block. The roof of the granny flat was made from tar drums which had been given to Reg by the storeman at APAC where Reg worked. Reg had to cut the top and bottom out of them and then flatten them out and get them corrugated to make them into a roof. During their time in this small house, Margaret, their second child, was born in April 1949. She was a blue baby and had to be sent to the Children's Hospital. She survived, though.

For a couple of years, Reg and Gwen couldn't get a permit to build the new house because the war restrictions were still in place. They finally got this permit and poured the house foundation in 1951. Reg was helped by Al, Trev, another friend Ray, and Gwen. They spent a full day with a mixer and piles of sand and metal, mixing and pouring. Red bricks were purchased for the outer walls and freestone for the front wall. The freestone arrived in great big rocks: twelve ton of it. Reg was skilled but didn't know how to cut them to shape. Thankfully, a shopkeeper who had been a bricklayer came around one day and showed him how to do it. They bought three tons of cement and had it made into cement bricks which were then used for the interior walls.

During this building activity, Reg was on shift work. While he was at work, Gwen would get things ready for him so that he could build the next day. She would stack a pile of bricks for him which he would then turn into a wall, working from around 8 am till lunchtime. Reg would then rest until it was time to go to work at 3.30 pm. He would work until 12 midnight and then come home to bed. It took them over two years to complete the house. Reg made all the doors, the windows and their frames. Trev helped him put the roof on. In those days, the ground was new, and lots of vegetables were grown to augment finances.

Not long after they moved into the new house, Mum and I found ourselves looking for accommodation. The building in Commercial Road was sold and we didn't know where we could go. This was 1954 and I was in my mid-twenties. We had lived there for some eighteen years. Reg invited us to move into the granny flat at the back of their house. He had fixed it up and made a kitchen on the verandah side of the building. Now, it had two bedrooms, a bathroom, a laundry and toilet. We moved in. The new kitchen under the old verandah was where we ate our meals. We then had a lot to do with Reg, Gwen and their two girls since we lived on the same block.

Reg couldn't do anything wrong, according to Gwen. As if in turn, Reg said that Gwen was always careful with their money, and because of her outlook on life and her saving habits, they always paid their bills as they arrived. They were happy. She could get moody — can't we all? If the back door was closed then you knew not to go in. We just didn't go in. But if the back door was open, well, that was different. When we used to do the sweet stalls for the Mission, Gwen and Mum would have a lovely time making sweets.

My older brother Reg was gruff. No getting around that. Mum would ask him if he would pick something up at the shop, and he would say 'No' without explanation. Half an hour later, he would be at the door asking what it was that Mum wanted there. Trevor was far more agreeable but it was not always the case that what he was asked to do got done. I once did a children's talk at church and used my two brothers to illustrate Jesus' story about the two sons in the vineyard. One was asked by their father to go out and work in the vineyard. He answered, 'No, I don't want to.' Later he thought better of it and went. The second son answered his father's request differently, 'Sure, I'll do that.' But he never did. That was Reg and Trev. One brother, Reg, couldn't let anyone think that he was kind but was always there. While the other brother was very kind – and Trev was – but frequently got diverted. I had a lot of time for them both, but you could always rely on Reg.

Trev had a girlfriend, Vera, when he was young. They were sweethearts. I was often sent out with them as a chaperone. I was six years younger than Trev and had to wait outside the gate while he kissed her good night. I was undoubtedly even less appreciated as a third person than I was at the cinema with Al and Evelyn some years earlier. The mother of the girl didn't like Trev at all so that when he went to the war, she encouraged Vera to go out with an older, more settled man who had better prospects. They married and had three sons. He was a shoemaker.

Trev met Elaine. When they married they were both Methodists. They had four children. Trev's work caused him to travel around the state quite a bit. How that affected the marriage, we don't know. But things broke down and they divorced. Whatever happened, it wasn't amicable; it was bitter. It seems after that, a friend got into Elaine's ear and she became a Jehovah's Witness (known as JWs). She would go around with Malcolm, the youngest child, and say she was a widow: she was a widow, she was sad, and she had this little boy. We found out about this and we were very upset. I suppose it reflected on us. We were family and only too willing to support her in any way we could. All the kids became Jehovah's Witness adherents.

Elaine wouldn't let us have anything to do with the children when she and Trev got divorced. Mum wasn't allowed to see her grandchildren. It hurt her terribly. Mum would get me to take her up to their place, since I had my driver's licence, to give birthday presents to the grandchildren. But upon arrival, the children were 'never home'. They were always sent out because they knew Grandma was coming. Many years later, I was telling Bernadette, Trev's oldest daughter, who had left the JWs, how much it hurt my mum. She said, 'Aunty Ruth, we never even knew Grandma came. And we never got the presents.' We always left presents for the kids — birthday and Christmas. They never knew that we came to see them. It's a wonder that they want to connect with me now. But they do. Anyway, it's lovely. Just lovely. But it was terribly sad then and really hurt Mum.

The eldest son and youngest girl stayed JW. The eldest daughter Bernadette became disenchanted and youngest boy Malcolm did, too, and they both left. Bernadette and

## PORT ADELAIDE 1945-1960 — WORKING AND WAITING

Malcolm had contact with their dad later in life. The other two remained JWs and were at Trev's funeral. They came up and gave me a big hug and said, 'Aunty Ruth, we do miss being a family.' I hadn't had contact with them due to their religion. Bernadette and Malcolm were the two who came to my 90th birthday party. They have stayed in touch with me. Bernadette comes and sees me two or three times a year. We have afternoon tea together and she always brings me muffins. We have become very good friends. Malcolm, the youngest, promised to come and sharpen the knives as a birthday present. He did that last year and that was lovely.

Trev married again. She was a nice lady with one son. They were together about five years when she became ill, went to hospital and died. I never met the son. We never saw them since they were mostly in the country. But some years after William died, I had to get the back part of the house here in Cheltenham renovated, to let more light in. It meant getting the wall on the eastern side rebuilt. The builder I had contracted had, in turn, employed a young brickie to do this work. We were talking one morning and something came up about him being a Fewster. I said, 'Fewster! Where do you fit in?' He said, 'Oh, Mum married Trevor Fewster.' Good grief! Meeting him was one of the biggest shocks of my life. He was virtually my nephew. We had a great talk. I saw him again at Trevor's funeral. Trev was his stepfather but he changed his name to Fewster. Then after both his mother and Trev died, he changed his name back to what it was before.

Trev was married three times, not two. Sometime after the death of his second wife, Trev heard that his childhood sweetheart, Vera, was in hospital. He visited her and they got back together and eventually got married. This was a happy marriage. She had known tragedy, though. One of the three sons she had from her first marriage drowned one Christmas Day. After that, she wouldn't have anything to do with Christmas for a few years. But by the time she got back with Trev, she had recovered. Vera was lovely. They had so much joy together. *Laugh*. She would laugh her head off. We always said that they were meant for each other. The funny part about all of this — like a postscript, I suppose — was a remark made by her mother who couldn't stand Trev when he was young. When she got old, she was in care in a nursing home. Trev used to take Vera to see her. During one such visit, the mother said to them both, 'I don't know why you two didn't get married in the first place.'

Trev told me later, 'I felt like saying, 'You silly old bitch, it was you that stopped us getting married in the first place.' So here was a love that endured and eventually found its place in my brother Trevor's life. We were so happy for him after all that heartache.

## PORT ADELAIDE 1945-1960 — WORKING AND WAITING

Apart from my work at Port Carriers, I was busy in the church — the Wesleyan Methodist Church in Port Adelaide. In those days, we had Sunday schools with large numbers of children and youth. I found myself becoming a spokesperson and advocate for them. The young people badly wanted to have some dancing at their socials, but I couldn't get the leaders of the church to agree. I persisted and persisted. It took years but eventually they said that we could have dancing, providing we had more games than dances. It seems a mundane sort of victory now but at the time it was hard work.

As in most institutions, it was the men in the Methodist church who held power. Reverend McCutcheon, our minister, was a great fellow. He did a lot of good work but he was a dictator. If he decided something would happen, then it happened, and it didn't matter what you said. But I just kept at it — wore him down, I suppose. It was the same with the Sunday school picnic. I managed to get church leaders to agree to allow the Sunday school's annual picnic to be held in the Hills, rather than the usual Outer Harbour reserve. To be able to take a day trip to the Hills was a rarity and a treat during those days. I felt for the young people. It seemed that they were always hampered.

After my sister and brothers were all married, Mum and I spent a lot of time together. The conclusion of a visit to Mum's relatives in Broken Hill was reported in the *Barrier*

*Daily Truth*, Wednesday 26th April 1950. I was twenty-one and in the social pages.

*Miss Ruth Fewster, who has been spending a holiday in Broken Hill for the first time with her uncle and aunt (Mr. and Mrs. Lance Dansie) and cousins Max and Morrie, left by Monday's plane for Adelaide accompanied by her mother (Mrs. Hubert Fewster).*

Mum once told me that she had Dad's grave dug twice as big because, she added, 'If Trevor hasn't got anywhere to be buried, he can have the other half of the grave.' There were so many things that I watched pass by my understanding without asking, 'Where did that come from?' For instance, why was Mum taking responsibility for Dad's burial? It wasn't as if she had anything to do with him. They were very much estranged. And at times, although not frequently, her bitterness surfaced.

Another of Mum's observations that escaped me at the time was, 'He said that he always wanted a little girl of his own.' I am sure now that Mum was trying to tell me something important. Back then, I didn't see or even question its possible significance. My response was, 'Well, if he wanted a little girl so badly why did he leave me?'

One time before I was married, Mum went to a couple of sessions at a church around the corner on Cheltenham Parade. The Salvation Army had a series of tent meetings.

Mum had been a Salvo before she married Dad. When she came home from one of these sessions, she said to me, 'I want to be baptised.'

I responded with, 'Oh you can't do that, Mum. You've been baptised. Everybody's baptised when they're babies. You can't be baptised again. You can only do it once.' She didn't enlighten me that the Salvation Army didn't baptise in general, let alone baptise children. Instead, she left it at that, not saying anything further, simply because I had said that she couldn't be baptised. I felt bad about it afterwards because if she really needed to, what did it matter?

I think she went ahead and did it anyway. She came home the next night in an uplifted sort of mood while maintaining a sense of quiet within herself. I've thought ever since that she'd secretly done it without me knowing.

I was going out with William in my early twenties. Mum thought William was a funny little man. And she was not referring to his sense of humour. He was short and so was I. He was 5 foot 4 inches (164 centimetres) tall and I was 5 foot 1. I just fitted under his arm. As I said earlier, in terms of my personhood, he was my balance. It's not that he couldn't be serious, but he could see the funny side of things. I couldn't think of anyone else who I wanted to be with. He had urticaria — hives. His lips and eyes would swell. He was affected by seafood. The first time I saw him with it, his eye was almost closed. 'What's wrong?' I asked. He had to explain to me that he had this complaint. He was very embarrassed.

We discussed our future together. He said that he thought that twenty-five would be a good age to get married. He was ten years older than me. When I turned twenty-five and raised the idea of marriage once again, he said, 'Oh, I'm not ready to get married.'

I was devastated. I went home in a kind of apoplectic state. I didn't let William know how I felt. That night when I went to bed, I cried and cried. I was sitting up in bed sobbing my heart out, as quietly as possible, mind you, since my mother was asleep in the other bed. This continued for some time. I became more and more distressed. A vision came to me. A man dressed in white stood in the bedroom doorway and, without speaking, communicated to me that everything would be all right. I became calmer and eventually went to sleep.

I never told anybody about the vision in case they thought I was either unhinged or too religious in that overly spiritual way. Nevertheless, I took great heart from that vision. And I would need to, for it would be another fifteen years before William and I married. Years later, I told William how distraught I had become at that time, and he said, 'Why on Earth didn't you tell me?' But I could have also asked him, 'How was it that you didn't ask me how I was feeling at the time?'

CHAPTER SIX

# Port Adelaide 1960-1982 — The Second Secret

While I was waiting for William, I got on with other things. Several times I got to a stage of saying, 'If he's not going to get married, I'm going to give him up.' I remember, one night, kneeling in the bath crying, 'I'm sick of this.' But then I'd think, 'I can't do without him.' I'd then go back into my shell and wait for something to happen. I knew he was the only one I wanted to be with, and that was the problem.

I had a small diversion before we were engaged. There was a young man from Queensland that I'd met up there when I was twenty-three. We kept in touch and he came down to see me in Adelaide. By then, I was nearly thirty. William got a bit of a shakeup that time because I was quite fond of Len. We were very good friends but not right for marriage. I would have needed to leave Mum and go to Queensland because Len wouldn't have moved here. So, there was no point. Len was disappointed that it didn't go further. We stayed close friends. We used to write to each other.

I went to a conference in Melbourne. Len happened to be in Melbourne at the time and he took me out to dinner before I went to the plane. It was getting later and later, and I was starting to get worried, 'How far is it to the airport?'

'Oh, don't worry we'll get you there in time.' Well, we didn't get there in time. We got there in time to see the plane go. I had to ring Mum and William who were down at the airport in Adelaide waiting for me: 'I'm sorry I missed the plane.' Len had to find a hotel for me to stay.

William was not happy: 'That bloomin' Lennie, I knew he'd make you miss the plane.'

Years later, Len was sick with oesophageal cancer. I said to him, 'I think I need to see you again.' William had passed away by then. I went up in the January before he died and stayed with them.

His wife was lovely and said, 'You married a man older than yourself and looked after him. Now I've married Len, and I'm looking after him.'

Len's mum had once said to me, her message and her grammar both mixed, 'You'd make a lovely wife for Len if you *wasn't* so old.' I was only three years older than him! During that visit, we had lovely conversations about how we had felt about each other over the course of our lives.

I happened to mention to him that I'd never had a Valentine's Day card. It must have been Valentine's Day the next day. So early the next morning, Len got in the car (he hadn't been driving because of his illness) and went to a stationer's. He bought me a Valentine's Day card. Before I had gotten out of bed, he opened the bedroom door and lobbed it onto the bed. He made sure that I got one before he died.

I had risen through the ranks of the Methodist Girls' Comradeship as I completed various stages of service. One early role was Minister of the Word within the local branch. This involved leading devotions at times and having a pastoral care role for the girls. Then I became Secretary and eventually the Director of the Port Adelaide Branch. After that, they asked me to be District Director which required my visiting and supporting Comrades in various churches and their branches around Adelaide, visiting them sometimes three or four nights a week. During such visits, I had to give a message of exhortation. I would also conduct conferral ceremonies where I presented Second and Third Degree badges to girls who had achieved particular service or learning tasks. After becoming District Director, I was State Director for two years and, following that period of service, I was invited to be General Superintendent for Australia for the three years between 1960 and 1963.

When I was General Superintendent, I had to visit every state. I didn't get to Western Australia. I didn't have time. However, I did a trip that started in Cairns and hopped down the east coast all the way down to Tasmania. I flew, making stops in Cairns, Brisbane, Sydney, Melbourne, and Hobart. In Cairns alone, I had to attend two or three different functions. It was a whirlwind three weeks. I had to preach at each place among my other ceremonial and pastoral duties. I took a long time to recover from that trip because I had travelled from hot places to really cold ones in a short period of time without really acclimatising to any of them. It was freezing in Tasmania. I couldn't get warm. It was a good experience anyway. Then for three years, I was what they called the past General Superintendent. It was a bit like a winding down of duties. I had just finished all of that when William and I got married in 1969.

In the years that I was General Superintendent, there were something like 15,000 people in the Methodist Girls' Comradeship organisation for whom I had overall responsibility. Then in the late '60s, Comrades seemed to reach its use-by date. Methodist Youth Fellowship became more popular and grew. The Comradeship dwindled since the Methodist Youth Fellowship was a mixed group of males and females. I remained in the Comradeship until it wound down.

I made some great friends from that time. There was a small group who were all past General Superintendents and we would go to the Adelaide Repertory Theatre productions together. It was an amateur theatre company but had significant support from actors such as Keith Michell. The Rep performed at many venues around Adelaide. Given our shared connection with Comrades, I called our little group 'The Pasties'. Later we had the 'Merry Widows' group which consisted of a group of us from church whose husbands had passed away. I had to give each group a name. I can't stand things without names. Two of us 'Pasties' went to England and Europe together, where amongst other things, we went to the Bavarian village of Oberammergau and saw their famous Passion Play. We were billeted in the village and on our beds were pillows that had been fashioned into butterfly shapes.

I was still working for Port Carriers in 1966. Two of Mr Good's nephews bought the transport part of the business. It was a transport and customs agent business. After that, it became Koch Transport, and I went with the transport side of the business. I had been with Port Carriers for about twenty-four years. I stayed with Koch Transport for another three years. The boss who was my line manager, died unexpectedly. He had a heart attack and so I became the secretary of the company. It was a demanding role having to ensure that the decisions of the board were implemented as well as overseeing the company's compliance with all the relevant regulatory requirements.

In that same year, Mum announced to the family that we were all going up to the Hills to celebrate Dad's birthday. We were all puzzled by this, but Mum insisted. We were going to celebrate his 70th birthday.

Dad had owned a shop in Adelaide for a while. It was in Dudley Park somewhere — a grocery shop. I don't know where exactly. He eventually sold the shop and went to Blackwood where he lived with his brother Harry and this lady, Bonnie, whom he had become involved with in Warooka. The three of them lived there together. Maybe it was a threesome, a menage-a-trois. Anyway, we all went up to Blackwood on this occasion. Trev might have been away, travelling for work. He didn't go. But the rest of us went and we all contributed towards the purchase of a watch as a present. We also bought a cake.

Well, that was another uncomfortable evening. I had been going out with William for some time. He accompanied us and, naturally enough, he had no shortage of funny observations to make about our visit afterwards. Dad was pleased we'd all come. But I never could understand why Mum insisted we all go when there'd been no contact for such a long time. Mum must have had her reasons but they were never explained to us.

The next time we saw Dad, he was in the Repatriation Hospital at Daw Park. This was a hospital for war veterans. It was just before he died. Mum, William and I went to visit him. I can remember Dad showing me his ankles because they were all swollen.

I had hoped that he would not be with us when I got married. Isn't that a terrible thing to say? I knew he would want to give me away at the wedding. And if he'd asked to do it, I couldn't have said 'no' because he was my father.

Dad didn't have much when he died. I doubt that he had any money. We just received his tools and his Bible and those sorts of things.

In 1965, I turned thirty-six. William and I had been going together for sixteen years. He was hit by another car while driving to work one morning. He was accompanied in the car by his niece Erica. Both were injured and taken to hospital. William had concussion and bruises while Erica had bruised knees and cuts.

In the accident, the contents of the car boot spilled all over the road. Among them was a quantity of plastic eggs which William had not yet removed after they had been used for an egg and spoon race at the Sunday school picnic. A small crowd had gathered at the accident and kept wondering why, when the cars ran over the eggs, nothing came out of them. Another item which William carried everywhere was a kitbag containing precious papers and share certificates. These were also strewn over the road. Fortunately, William's brother had been following in his own car on his way to work and saw the kitbag. He retrieved it and the papers, much to William's relief.

This accident was a catalyst that stirred us into realising that we did not want to be without each other and so we became engaged. The night this happened, William said, 'Now we must look for somewhere to live.'

I replied, 'Oh! Let me enjoy being engaged first.' Big mistake! We both settled back and it was four more years before the next step happened.

We became exceptionally close after the accident. William was calling in on his way to work, driving down from the city to Port Adelaide to have lunch with me then driving back to work, calling in to see me on his way home from work, going to his brother's place for his evening meal and then coming back for the evening. It all became too much for my mother. One night she let burst, 'For goodness sake! Isn't it time you two got married?'

So we did! He was fifty and I was forty. We had been going together for twenty years. And these twenty would be followed by fifteen years of good marriage. It was 1969. William was in his thirties when they discovered that he had nephritis and his kidneys were failing. I think that this was why he was a little afraid of getting married. He wasn't sure that he wanted to have children with that complaint.

Evelyn helped me greatly in the planning of my wedding. I flipped my plans for a wedding dress and a going-away frock. I had originally intended to have my wedding dress made and buy my going-away frock. In the end, I did it the other way 'round. I had my going away frock made and bought my wedding dress. I hadn't felt that I could spend the amount that a wedding dress was going to cost me. Evelyn said, 'Why don't we go and look?' We did that and found a wedding dress we both really liked. She encouraged me to buy it.

The wedding gown was a plain frock with a coat that went over and lace that went all the way around the front to the sleeves. It was lovely. And it was something I could afford. But the lady in the shop was most upset because there was a long train on the coat and I didn't feel it was appropriate for a forty-year-old. I asked them to cut off some of the train. She wasn't at all happy about that. Evelyn also wanted me to have it a bit longer than I did. I had it the length I wanted it.

A sister-in-law on William's side (his brother's wife) said to me, 'You're too old to be a bride.'

But Mavis, William's sister, countered that, 'Don't take any notice of her. If you want to be a bride, be a bride.' I had my wedding photos taken in the front room of Reg and Gwen's house. Evelyn made my wedding cake, and Mavis iced it just as effectively as she had 'iced' the you're-too-old-to-be-a-bride comment.

William was baptised as an infant in the Church of England. When he came back from the war, he wasn't a regular churchgoer. But he was quite accepting of the fact that I was very involved in the church. I happened to be in the district choir for Port Adelaide for a production of *Handel's Messiah*. I wanted him to come. His sister-in-law talked him into coming with her so that he didn't have to go on his own. I think that was mainly the problem: he did not want to go to things where he didn't know people. I can understand that. He was shy with people he didn't know, although he was very forthcoming with anybody he did know. He teased the life out of my mother. She jumped every time. He could get a rise out of Mum quite easily. He teased the life out of me too. When he lost a lot of his ability after he had his stroke, the family thought he was coming good because he started teasing me once more.

I got William to come to some other special event at the Methodist church in Dale Street before we joined with the

Congregationalists. He got to know a couple of people, and then he started to come to church with me. He wouldn't come at night because he liked to go to his brother's place on Sunday night for tea, but he would come in the morning. Then he started coming with me at night, and occasionally, I would go to his brother's for tea on Sunday night. We compromised there. Then they asked him to go on the board of the Mission. From then on, he felt that he had a role to play and his faith deepened to the point where, after he had his stroke and couldn't talk, I said to him, 'William, do you still believe in Jesus?'

He launched his reply at me, 'Course! Yes!' As much to say, 'Stupid question.' He couldn't say many words, but even though he'd been through all that, he still had his faith. That was a great thing for me because he'd started off being very lukewarm. His faith grew through our association. We were both very committed to being Christian.

I continued to work with Koch Transport for a few years after I got married. It all got a bit hard. It was too big a job being secretary. William and I were going back after tea and doing work. He'd come with me because he didn't like me being in the building on my own. I was working Saturdays and Sunday afternoons. I managed it but it was hard work. When I told him I was leaving, the boss at Koch Transport wasn't very happy with me. He had only been managing the business for three years and he didn't want me to leave because I had all the experience. But it got too much for me. When I told the church I was leaving work, they approached me to be administrator of the church.

Not long after the Congregational and Methodist churches joined in Port Adelaide, the Methodist church in Dale Street was bulldozed. The day after, Mum and I stood in front of the rubble and cried. That church had been part of our lives all these years, supporting us and providing fellowship. At the time, the Superintendent of the Mission, Reverend George Martin, told me I could have anything I wished from the building. I chose two wrought iron bars that had been across the front doors of the church. We intended to put them on a wooden gate that we planned for our house in Cheltenham. We never got around to it and the bars still sit up on a bench in the shed. I also took two pieces of stonework from the curved gable. They still sit in the house here somewhere too. I suppose that they will eventually go into the hard rubbish collection.

Since I was now the administrator of the Methodist church, they gave me a seat on the deaconate. They had deacons in those days and they were like the church council. In other words, they ran the church. My having a seat in the deaconate did not go down too well with some of the elderly 'Cong' ministers because they'd never had a woman on there before. And then there was the fact that I was a Methodist.

One time, they were discussing the curriculum for the Sunday school. We had brought all our kids over from the Methodist church with us. I was running the primary school department of the Sunday school. When they were talking about the Sunday school curriculum, one of the deacons, John Cockington, said, 'I think we should stick with the Congregational material because that is our material.'

I replied, 'Well, the Methodist material is our material. We should be supporting our material.' He conceded this and we came to an arrangement for the Sunday school which was a conglomerate of both curricula.

The first event I had to organise in the Cong church was their Sunday school anniversary. It was very similar to ours in so much as they used to construct a big platform that went right up to the back wall of the church. We Methodists used to do that as well. Each department within the Sunday school had to produce something. I worked on the presentation of the primary school age group. I had a very large box which I'd painted red. Then I put the Bible on it. All the kids had to dress up in different garb or costume related to the Bible and emerge through this great big box and tell a part of the biblical story. I didn't know young Ian was dyslexic. I got him to say a little piece. He had the greatest difficulty learning it, but I kept encouraging him, and he persevered. On the day he came out of the box and just said his bit. I was very proud of him. I have been telling him all his life that I am so proud of him. I still get a hug from him most Sundays. And his campervan is parked in my carport because he doesn't have a place for it at his unit.

We were without a minister for twelve months and George Fleming, as secretary, virtually ran the church before Jim arrived as minister. Jim and I worked very well together but they didn't have an office for me. We both had to use his study. One day I arrived at work. He'd gone out and his dirty socks were on the desk. 'That's enough I can't stand it,' I thought. I packed up and came home.

Jim was very concerned that I'd disappeared. He suggested I have a talk with Laurie Mickan from Parkin Wesley, the place where they trained Methodist (and later Uniting Church) ministers. The first thing he told me was, 'You've got to get out of that study. You and Jim shouldn't be working in the same area. You both need your space.'

Jim and his wife Noelene had a closed-in porch and they turned it into an office for me. I could come in with my own key to my office. I was quite separate from the house. However, there were double doors that went into the bedroom from the office because it was actually a porch. I found that was a bit disconcerting because I had to go through their bedroom to get into the house to use the kitchen or toilet. Noelene was very cooperative, and she turned the bedroom into the dining room. I didn't then mind so much walking through the dining room to get to the kitchen. But it was still awkward because, although I could go into my own office, I felt as though I should tell Noelene I was in the house. I could open the office door and go in there, but then I still had to go through their house to get to the kitchen or toilet.

I was supposed to only work two days a week but I ended up working full time almost. They said that they could pay me $1000 towards my expenses — home phone and travel time and all that. That was for two days but the job got bigger. At one stage, because the job had expanded to five days a week, they decided to pay me $1,500, but William said, 'No.' He didn't want me to get any more money because it was going to affect his taxation. We considered that $500 as part of our offering to the church.

I did the administrator's job at the Port Church for ten years and became a thread of continuity for ministers of the church over the ensuing decade into the late '90s. After I finished as administrator, I became secretary. I was virtually still doing most of the previous duties but I was unpaid. But that was alright.

Mum and I used to cook coconut ice, fudge, jubes and other sweets to be sold as fundraisers for the work of the Mission in Port Adelaide. The first year, we made $5.80 because we were very new to it, but, towards the end, we were making hundreds. Our last stall made $500 so we really went out on a high note. Evelyn wasn't involved in that much. It was mostly Mum and I since we lived together. I used to work all day and then come home and cook sweets until midnight. My sister-in-law Gwen, who was nearby, used to make baskets for me for the fair. We started off with the participation of friends, Comrades, and the Evening Fellowship group from the church. I was convener, and Mum would do a lot of things for me in the daytime, then I would come home from work, and we would keep going.

Mum died in December of 1979. After William and I got married, she had stayed on in our little house at the back of Reg and Gwen's for some years. Then as she became more frail, she was cared for in Wesley House. In 1987, a new group home for older people in West Lakes was named Fewster Grove in recognition of our family's contribution to the Mission. I think Mum was gone by the time Fewster Grove was opened. I couldn't go to the opening, but Evelyn and Al, Reg and Gwen went as the Fewster family. They had me over at a later date to Fewster Grove for a special lunch.

When Mum went into care at Wesley House, if Evelyn wanted to take her out for the day, Mum often didn't have time. She had too many things to do in Wesley. She had friends, and other things were happening. But if I wanted to take her out, she was always available. Evelyn didn't feel good about that. She felt that Mum didn't want to be with her, but I really don't think it was that. I think it was more that Mum had made a circle of friends. I used to take her out on a Wednesday. I always had a regular day. Then Evelyn would want to take her out on Thursday but she had been out on Wednesday. I think that it hurt Evelyn. She felt Mum didn't want to go with her. Still, Mum did go to Evelyn's place quite a lot. That was the situation: she was never 'not available' for me, but she could be 'not available' for Evelyn.

It was 1982. Evelyn came to see me out of the blue. One of our uncles had died. It was one of Dad's stepbrothers, a son of Grandfather's second wife, dear Gran, who we used to visit at Corny Point. Because he died intestate, the money was to be divided between all the nieces and nephews. So, we all received something. However, Evelyn wasn't listed as Dad's daughter on any document. On her birth certificate, it had 'father unknown'. There was some hassle, therefore, about whether she should be included in this disbursement of money. I could not understand what the problem was until one day, Evelyn came to me in tears. 'I have something to tell you,' she said. 'I am not really your sister. Your father is not my father. I've never told you because I thought you mightn't love me.'

My response was, 'Oh Evelyn! It makes me love you all the more. If Dad had not accepted you as his daughter, I would never have had a sister.' She told me what she knew about Mum's story. We spent a long time together assuring each other of our love. She and I were already very close, and we only became closer after that.

I wish they had told me before Evelyn had to because I would have had a much kinder feeling towards my father. From another angle, my mother had a terrible inferiority complex, and I am sure it was because of this business. As an eighteen-year-old, she was working as a housemaid because that's all she was equipped to do. She was from a family of thirteen children, and they didn't have any money to be training their kids to do things. She was working as a housemaid and, in those days, the master of the house felt he had the 'right' to everybody. I learned that was how she became pregnant. After that, she went to stay with her sister so that she was out of the community.

Mum had always been our rock. She was truly brilliant at helping us through problems. It was as if, when looking at us, she had clarity and conviction, but when looking inward, she only found insecurity and doubt about the worth of her own decisions.

CHAPTER SEVEN

# The First Garden Story

The cart outside the gate at the head of the driveway seemed to beckon visitors to the garden. When those who walked by saw fresh produce on the cart — tomatoes, lettuce, capsicums, spinach, sweet potatoes and beetroot, or whatever was in season — they generally wanted to be sure it was free for the taking, and this involved some kind of verbal exchange. Sometimes, they would then walk down the drive into the garden itself. One time, a young guy came in and saw a couple of the gardeners digging in the new garden bed where the old hall had been demolished. He asked if he could join in.

'I live in Blair Athol but got some troubles there and am just staying in the Port for a bit. I wouldn't mind a bit of exercise. I've been cooped up in a room for a few days.'

He picked up a spare spade and starting digging alongside them. They were digging out remnant stone and bricks left over from the demolition, and he asked them, 'What do you do here?'

Todd pointed to a native pine — the Bent Pine — that grew beside the driveway near the middle of the garden. It was bent over almost at a right angle to the ground. He said to the young guy, 'See that tree. That gives us the name of the garden. It's like our motto. It says to us that no matter what life has thrown at you, and whatever shape you are in now, it is still possible to have a place where you can grow and be healthy.'

The young guy answered, 'Shit yeah. That's so true.'

Garden church was a form of Sunday worship which had developed since the community garden started up three years earlier. How it came to have its place on the worship roster was not clear in Todd's memory. It may have expressed an openness to new ideas by the congregation or it might have served the purpose of filling a gap in the worship roster — a three-month table of dates, lectionary readings and otherwise empty boxes which was proving, over time, more difficult to populate. Maybe both explanations were true.

Garden church took place about once a quarter. The gardening team emphasised that garden church wasn't so much church out-in-the-garden, it was worship that made use of the activities and images that were part of the life of the garden: the planting of seed, the growing, pruning, and harvesting of fruit and vegetables, followed by the sharing of produce with neighbours and passers-by. The congregation, including its older members, really enjoyed being outside in the garden on a Sunday morning. If it was winter and cold the chairs would be placed on the pavers just behind the church in the warming sun. If it was hotter they would be set out under the plane trees and their deep shade.

The sounds of Port Adelaide — the thrum of traffic, the sirens from passing emergency vehicles and the train whistles from the rail museum just across the road — filtered into the quietness of prayer. These intrusions seemed to enhance rather than distract from worship. Now that the back area behind the church was so verdant, it attracted even more 'rough sleepers' than usual. One time, the Bent Pine crew had to let some of these transient residents know that worship was going to be 'just feet away' and not to be surprised either by the singing or the greater number of voices than they were used to out there, in the quiet of the garden. The sounds of the Port and the presence of our guests were all reminders of where we were and where we should be: neighbours in the local community rather than worshippers hidden inside the fine building.

At garden church there was not the traditional twenty-minute sermon. Worship was largely enacted in the common gardening tasks mentioned above. The churchgoers were, depending on the time of the year, out of their chairs and in the garden planting, pruning, weeding or watering.

Or even just spending time looking at things. After that, there was time for prayer, a song and a homily of just a few minutes. Todd took his turn at giving the homily despite his reluctance to now participate in worship inside the church. As a teacher, he liked mulling over texts and figuring out what they had to say, firstly to him, and then to others. He still held on to the belief, without much conviction, that he did have something to say. Maybe it was the teacher in him that told him so. Anyway, as a minimal outcome, he thought that by doing this, his non-participation 'inside' the church was somehow softened.

Todd had been reading some work from Howard Thurman about the First Garden Story in Genesis, the book at the start of the Bible — the one where Adam and Eve eat the forbidden fruit and the woes of humanity supposedly begin. Thurman, who was a spiritual mentor to the American civil rights leader, Martin Luther King Jr, provided new insights for Todd on this First Garden Story.

In his reflection on what happened in the First Garden story, Thurman did not focus on humankind's disobedience to God in eating the fruit from the tree of knowledge. Instead, he wrote that with the coming of knowledge there was also the loss of innocence. Adam and Eve (and presumably the rest of us), now driven from the garden, had to assume responsibility for their own lives.

Outside, in the Bent Pine garden, Todd spoke to the congregation in the manner of a preacher but, at the same time, he was in private conversation, trying to answer his own questions about the direction of his faith.

The First Garden Story continues to play out in each of our lives. As we grow into the world, we learn things that are good and necessary to grow up. However, a knowledge of the 'good' is accompanied by the learning of other things – one might say a 'knowledge of evil':

We see things that we would rather not have seen.

We hear things that we would rather not have heard.

We experience things that we would rather not have experienced.

With such knowledge, innocence is lost. And yet, Jesus says in the Gospel of Matthew, 'Unless you change and become like little children you will never enter the Kingdom of Heaven.' He issues a radical, almost preposterous, call for us to return to innocence.

But can we really become like little children with their innocence?

How can we 'unsee' what we have seen?

How can we 'unhear' what we have heard?

How can we 'un-experience' what we have experienced?

Jesus also said, 'Come to me, all who labour and are heavy laden, and I will give you rest.' What we have learned is a heavy knowledge, and we carry it uneasily. It includes all that we have seen, heard and experienced: that we have done to others and that which has been done to ourselves. We find ourselves on a quest to mitigate the damage it has wrought, seeking to become once more 'unharmed' by what we know. It is a quest because we can never really go back – not to the garden, at least, for we have been driven out. And we are not completely sure of the way forward. But we must go on. We are responsible for our own lives.

Which way from the Garden — the Desert or the City? Jesus went to both. He also went back to the garden, the Garden of Gethsemane, on the last evening of his life. He tried to find solace there in his anguish and fear of what the following day would hold for him. Desert, City, Garden — where should we be? We try to follow Him to each place:

To help create spaces where people can belong, grow, and even flourish, despite the weathering life has wrought on them or in them — like the bent-over native pine that gives its name to our garden.

To welcome others and look past their asymmetries and flaws even as we hope that they might do so for us.

When Todd and I met on our semi-regular Thursday afternoon the following week, Todd asked me whether he could share something of his family background. He told this story.

'You were in your early fifties, Ruth, when you first learned of your sister Evelyn's secret. My father didn't find out his family secret — namely, that his older sister was, in fact, his mother — until he was in his late fifties. In her late teens, she had become pregnant outside of marriage. Like Mabel, and at about the same age, she withdrew from open society to have the child because of the stigma. My dad was then brought up by her parents, his grandparents. That a marriage did not take place as it commonly did when other young couples 'jumped the gun' was possibly because one family was from an Anglican background and the other family was Catholic.

'My father always said that he was very well looked after and cared for. There was the occasional clue, though: he had always wondered at a certain distance that existed between him and his 'parents', one that did not seem to exist with other children and their parents. Ironically, Dad's mother and father overcame previous hurdles and eventually married. The puzzling thing was that after they did this, they still didn't break the secret that the youngest member of the family was in fact their boy. And so, the scenario played out over decades and not without its adverse effects. Even when my father, a fighter pilot, was shot down in the war and taken to a POW camp, his real parents could not let on that he was their son. They must have suffered terribly. The holding of the secret took its toll on my grandmother. She had an underlying and excoriating anger that found its way off its tight leash at times.

'They had another child, a daughter, on the "right side of the blankets", as they used to say then. Sadly, this girl bore the brunt of her mother's anger at times. The daughter had mental health problems as she grew up. Fortunately, she met and married a very kind and compassionate man and was happy for periods of time. But when it came her turn to have children, two of them, she could not love them, not well, at least, and not like their father did. He died when the children were adults, and the chasm left in their lives by his passing was immense.

'Just as the mechanism that broke the seal on Evelyn's secret came in a belated and unexpected manner, so too did it happen with my father. Dad's sister — as they still knew her to be — would come over every year from Sydney and spend Christmas and January with Mum and Dad. One year, as it happened, Dad required a birth certificate in order to get a passport — he had been invited to be part of a healthcare team to go to Cambodia after the fall of Pol Pot. The letter from the registrar of Births, Deaths and Marriages never arrived. Actually, it did, but it had been intercepted at the letterbox by Dad's sister. On the day she was due to fly back to Sydney, she gave it to my mother (Dad must have been at work). All she said was, 'Tell Alan I always loved him.' And there it was, Dad's sister was his mother.

Mum and Dad would have been only too happy to recognise, and even celebrate, this new relationship. And that's what they told her. But Dad's mother could not. She would never speak of it again. And neither did she ever come and stay with Mum and Dad again, although they did visit her in Sydney.'

Todd and I continued to talk about it. I told him, 'Oh yes, it was like that then. Often, we just didn't say what needed to be said. It was a time when we believed that the best way forward was to accept one's lot and just get on with it.'

Todd then observed, 'I see that what happened to your mother, Ruth, was like a re-enactment of the First Garden Story in that she experienced a harsh and unjust 'knowledge' of the world, lost her innocence, and had to become responsible for her life and the lives of her children. It was obviously a bitter experience, having to carry the weight of her secret, for both herself and her oldest daughter. She must have wondered, at times, how it was all going to work out. I like to think that she later experienced a way back to the Garden to find a place of healing, and to undo the damage done to her.

'For me, your story is an opportunity to witness a healing which was not evident in my grandmother's story.

Here, there is the possibility of grace. I think it is a story that could encourage others.'

I listened to Todd's words and weighed them up, 'Todd, I do see what you are saying, and if it was only me that I had to think about, I would have no hesitation. This idea excites me. But I have to think about my niece and nephew (Evelyn's children) and what they would have to say. Let me ponder on it for a while.'

CHAPTER EIGHT

# Cheltenham 1984-2010 — Passings

William's health began to seriously deteriorate in the same year Mum passed on — 1979. He had to retire from work as his complaint worsened. He was sixty. He went on to have dialysis three times a week over the next three and a half years. This was happening at the time Evelyn disclosed her secret to me. We continued to see each other a lot, but I was also preoccupied with looking after and supporting William. Then he had a stroke – a massive stroke. He lost the use of his right arm and leg and his speech. Losing speech was the hardest, but I could usually work out what he wanted. We'd known each other for that long. It was most difficult for him in conversation with other people when he wanted to contribute and couldn't.

As far as his wants and his needs, I could work that out. We used to go to water therapy at Mac's pool up on Victoria

Road five times a week. If Jill, William's niece, wasn't on duty she would come with me. She was a nurse. William loved being in the water. I was young enough to look after him which was good.

We used to take trays of nectarines from our trees to Dr Barrett with whom we became very friendly. One day we didn't have any nectarines and William badly wanted to go and buy some grapes and a rockmelon to take. We were running late and I said we didn't have time. We were arguing about it as I drove. William was becoming quite distressed, and I didn't notice a school crossing and drove straight through at speed. A policeman was behind me and pulled us over. He wouldn't accept my explanation and I received a substantial fine.

At a certain point after his stroke, it was decided to halt William's dialysis and this had a finality to it. William died in 1984. I remember his last night. He had short periods of wakefulness but was mostly in a fitful sleep. At one point he opened his eyes and focussed on me with an overwhelming intensity and longing — 'Drink to me only with thine eyes.' That expression of love was our last moment together.

I was still involved in the church. I am sure that my work there, and the fellowship of friends at church, got me through the time after William's death. And, of course, my dear Evelyn. One of the things I hated doing was coming home to an empty house after I had been to lawn bowls. Bowls were on Thursdays. Evelyn invited me to come to her on Thursdays for tea each week. Al used to get 'toey' if I arrived past 5 pm as he was used to having his dinner at 4.45 pm.

Then I turned sixty and decided it was my time for travel. I went overseas two years in a row. I had a long-time friend, Pam, who had lived next door to us when we were children. I had pushed her in a stroller when I was ten years old. Pam and her husband Keith invited me to go on a world trip. Three people is not a good idea for prolonged travel. Well, at least, not a couple and a third person. We were away six weeks. Keith was inclined to be a bit bossy and I was used to being the boss all my life. We were having a meal and I said to Pam, who was being a bit obstreperous, 'For goodness' sake, Pam, grow up!'

He piped up, 'Don't speak to my wife like that!'

That didn't go down well with me. However, we managed to stay friends. At one stage, we had to share a bedroom. Our trip included Egypt, and a boat cruise down the Nile. Pam and Keith didn't take any notice of what they were told regarding the importance of only drinking filtered water and not cleaning teeth using local water. They paid the consequences and were otherwise engaged during this boat cruise. Meanwhile, I enjoyed sitting in the boat and watching rural Egypt slide by. It was just wonderful. Another time, there was a trip to Canada with friends, (dirty-socks-on-the-desk)

Jim and Noelene. I also spent time in Dubai with Jill. She was a teacher in a nursing program there.

When I was young, the letter of the law was the thing. You followed what the Church told you was the way you should go. In the Methodist Church, you didn't dance, you didn't drink, you didn't gamble. Any one of these was very much something I would abhor, notwithstanding my battles with authorities to allow dancing at the church socials. When I started going out with William, he had a beer at some function we went to. I was absolutely horrified that he would do that, especially when he knew I was so much against it. But after a while, he accepted the fact that I didn't think it was the right thing to do and he didn't drink. Now, things have changed. I don't like to see people drink in excess, but if someone fancies a beer instead of a lemonade, then that's their prerogative. It doesn't affect the way I feel personally about my faith with the Lord. It's my faith in the Lord that's important, not how people behave.

Over the years, I have changed and the Church has too. I don't see the outright ill in some things I did when I was young. For instance, I can remember when I started playing bowls, I used to get terribly uncomfortable because they would come around with raffles all the time. I just couldn't take raffle tickets. It was something I just couldn't do. They used to tease me about it. One time I took a raffle ticket and felt as though I had crossed the line and was going to hell! Not really, but I was very uneasy about it. Gradually, I came to see that it was their way of raising money to keep the club going. One of the elderly ladies was always trying to get me to take raffle tickets, and when I finally took one, she was surprised. She said, 'There you go, you see.' I took that as meaning that she was pleased to see that I was normal. Here am I feeling terribly upset that I'd taken a raffle ticket and she's saying, 'That's good now. You've passed the pale.'

At the bowls club, they were always trying to get me to go to the Melbourne Cup Day, and I wouldn't go because all you did was gamble all day. But I must have relented at some stage, for the next thing this same woman did to me was make me pay out for our Melbourne Cup Day. I felt I needed to do it because it was a job I was being given on the day. Oh, it was the worst day of my life. I paid out all these people with their winnings. Afterwards I thought, 'Here we go again … It's not affecting my faith; it's not making me a wicked person. I'm helping raise money for the club.' So, I gave in. It didn't alter the fact that I loved the Lord. It didn't alter the fact that I wanted to be kind to people and I wanted to pray for people. It was a superfluous thing that didn't matter.

It was in the year 2000, around July, when Evelyn called me at 5 am one Sunday morning because she couldn't wake Al.

After I arrived, it was obvious we needed an ambulance, and Al was taken to hospital. We followed. I stayed with Evelyn until we returned home later in the day. After Al died, I lived with Evelyn for a fortnight until she felt comfortable staying at night on her own. I don't know that she ever felt comfortable again being alone.

It became a ritual for me to go for tea on Thursday nights and then stay over and go home on Friday morning. I often took takeaway fish and chips to save her cooking. Evelyn knew that I loved lemon fluff pudding, so almost every week, she would make one for dessert. Sometimes I knew it was a struggle for her, but she did it for me and I loved her so much for the effort. Although, I would have happily spared her the energy.

Sometimes I would go and watch the football with her. But she was a villain. The radio broadcast was always ahead of the TV. Even now I don't like to know the result ahead of time if I am watching. Evelyn couldn't bear to wait; she would sneak out to the kitchen and listen to the wireless. I would say, 'Don't tell me.' But if she came in with a grin all over her face, I knew we were winning.

Evelyn had her bunions operated on and she was very keen to get back into 'proper' shoes. Her feet were still painful but I drove her to town and we parked in the Adelaide Central Market carpark as the shop was in that part of town. How she suffered for style that day. Poor dear. In the end, it was just too painful for her to walk and we had to come home empty-handed.

As Evelyn got older, she looked so much like Mum. I used to call her Mum sometimes. She developed heart problems and had a pacemaker implanted. Sadly, dear Evelyn had a stroke some four days later. Just as Mum had, Evelyn went into care at Wesley House. She would be there for the next seven years. I visited her almost every day in those seven years.

One night, after she had her stroke, Evelyn said to me, 'Ruth, I have to tell you something that's going to upset you.'

'Oh, what's that?'

'Your dad was not your dad, you know.'

'No, dear. That was you.'

'No, dear. No, dear, it was you.'

Of course, I knew it wasn't me but she was convinced it *was* me who had a different father. I went racing home and rang my brother. I was in tears. 'Was my father my father?'

Reg, as usual, was to the point, 'Of course, he was your father. Don't be stupid! You know she's not well.'

I ended up in tears that night just because she told *me* my father was not my father. I had a small inkling of what she must have felt when she found out. Kaye, Evelyn's daughter, said that her mum had told her of the sleepless nights she had when she found out that Dad wasn't her father. She was terribly impacted. In the disorientation of her illness, she had tried to transfer her suffering to me. Not that I understood that at the time. Evelyn died in 2010. She was ninety-three, the age I am now. I miss her still.

Reg passed away on 16th September 2004. It was the day of his and Gwen's 60th wedding anniversary. He was eighty-four. Gruff old Reg had been more of a dad to me than Dad had.

Trev left us in 2014. Although we used to talk to each other at intervals and send Christmas and birthday cards, distance was always a deterrent to our meeting face-to-face. I was very pleased to have been able to share in his 90th birthday celebrations in 2013. They were held at Moonta on the Yorke Peninsula where he had been living with Vera.

Of my immediate family, now only I remain. I am well supported by my friends at church. In truth, I would say that my church family is just that. It is now my family. I still live in the house in Cheltenham where William and I spent our married life. I am independent, but in large part, this is because of the help of my friends from church. I also get a lot of support from Jill, William's niece, and have a long weekly phone call on Saturday afternoons with Kaye, Evelyn's daughter. She was named after me (middle name). Sadly, she is unwell.

A gardener comes once a week. This allows me to maintain my own garden and the several fruit trees that are in it.

I still like to make jam; fig and ginger being a favourite but apricot and marmalade get a guernsey as well. I sell them at church to augment the budget there. I receive some help with house cleaning. And then there is Kevin, my IT man. He is the son of a longstanding friend. He generously helps me with all my computer problems — and I do get stumped quite frequently, not just with the steps to carry out many of the functions on a computer, but also with recognising and dealing with the various scams that seem to flood my phone and internet communication. But it is good to be online. One of the things I really like about email is receiving photographs of grandchildren of friends of mine — these are younger friends from church.

Overall, I do quite okay in my wish to continue with an independent life. It was hard when I had to hand in my driver's licence a few years ago. I adapted. *Move on* is another of my mottos — even if this happens to be via taxi vouchers and lifts, courtesy of friends. I take myself shopping in the Port on Fridays, and afterwards, attend the creative arts session at the CK Community Hub in the afternoon. This is a shop in the centre of the Port which has been owned and operated by our church for four decades. I get to church most Sundays with Jane's help. She goes to the Port Church and lives nearby. She is just wonderful.

I often read the Bible readings and lead prayers. Learning how to make use of large print on my computer helps me prepare for doing this because of my deteriorating eyesight.

It is both pleasing and vexing to me that my office at home is a cluttered and busy space.

I remain as active as my health allows me, and I like to think that the pacemaker which I had implanted last year has to keep pace with me.

Our heritage listed church building still commands a presence in Commercial Road. But much has changed. Now our congregation is small and faces challenges. In its heyday, with the upstairs gallery, our church could seat up to 800 people. Now, our numbers are less than five per cent of that. Some of the young ones left about five years ago. We thought that it was just a matter of worship style. But no, it was less about that and more an appeal to take on the leadership of the congregation and create a church for contemporary times — at least as they saw it. Anyway, our decision led to what we had feared — the fragmentation of our congregation.

I've beaten myself up over that a few times. I used to champion the needs of the young people and here I had participated in stifling them. Must it be always like this with generational change? Had I become rigid like Reverend McCutcheon, the man I used to challenge on behalf of the youth? I like to think that it wasn't that. I made a mistake. I think that it was more a fault in my understanding of what they wanted.

I am more keenly aware of my mortality these days, and that sense is reinforced when I find myself writing eulogies for friends who have passed. Our congregation, and its existence in this lovely old church building, is also confronted with the notion of passing.

## CHAPTER NINE

# The End of Worlds

It was early spring. The congregation was outside in the sun. The night before, the Port Adelaide football team had beaten its cross-town rivals in the local 'showdown', and the mood of several in the congregation was upbeat. Beside the 'altar' which was the produce cart, tidied up, were various gardening implements. Watering cans, trowels, spades, pitchforks, and seedlings in small pots ready for planting lay in front of a bale of straw that would be teased apart and used for mulch.

On this day, having cleared the garden of the detritus of winter, the group was ready for spring planting. After thirty minutes of planting seedlings of beans, lettuce, spinach, kale, rhubarb, spring onions, cucumber and rockmelon, and then providing a cover of mulch for each, the congregation gathered once more.

The homily for the day alluded to the loss experienced by several of Todd's fellow church members in recent times.

There was the personal loss of partners and long-time friends. There was the incremental loss of capacities associated with declining health. Added to these was the threat, hanging over the congregation, of the looming loss of their fellowship or, at least, the meeting place for it.

An occupational health and safety inspection had been carried out on the church properties by synod. The inspectors noted property structures and items that required maintenance, grading these as either red (meaning urgent) or yellow (pending). The CK Community Hub was included in the report. Some of the maintenance needs, identified as red flag items, were quite expensive. Further to this, there was a recommendation to set up an annual maintenance fund. The amount suggested was not far south of the congregation's overall yearly budget — simply to address the projected maintenance needs.

The challenges were, therefore, occurring on two fronts: the church was facing significant issues of building maintenance and an ageing of leadership and volunteers. More and more required 'doing' with less and less capacity for doing it.

Todd entitled this homily, *The End of Worlds*.

> With their beginnings and endings, there are parallels between the seasons out here in the garden and the liturgical seasons observed inside the church.
>
> Sometimes, more rarely, we are constrained to take an even wider view of our existence here.

Imagine a drone above us — an overview taking in this church and garden sitting in this part of Port Adelaide. It is a grand sight. If the drone could also provide a historical view, we would see, not more than 400 metres from here, the first chapel used by the Congregational church in Port Adelaide, situated on the corner of Lipson and St Vincent streets. On 30th April 1866, it burned down.

*Our Scotch friends kindly gave us the use of their first chapel. The late Mr William Blackler generously offered us the use of his store, and services were held there for some weeks until we moved into the town hall, which had only recently been built. There we stayed for about six months ... [before] ... transferring the services to the Oddfellows Hall, and there we remained until we moved into the third and present church.*[1]

All things have their time and then pass and, in turn, new possibilities or opportunities emerge. The Congregationalists were sojourners for a period and things eventually worked out for them right here.

We know, however, that the church is not just about buildings. In each of our personal lives, too, there are inescapable passings (with a sense of being uprooted) and there are beginnings (sometimes

---

1 From a 'Narrative sketch of the foundation and early history of the Port Adelaide Congregational Church', p16.

unwanted) bringing the need for new starts. These are also like the change of seasons.

The Franciscan scholar Richard Rohr tells us how both 'prophecy' and 'apocalypse' in scripture have been largely misinterpreted. They have come to be understood as referring to the future (prophecy) or 'end of time' events (apocalypse). But prophetic and apocalyptic scripture both describe and make comment on the present. Prophets in the Bible spoke out, often at great peril to themselves, of the need for people to turn around and behave differently based on present events and actions. Likewise, the apocalyptic literature uses graphic imagery to break into our habits of mind and rigid thinking to uncover or unveil a present reality. (The New Testament books of Mark and Revelation contain examples.) Richard Rohr says, 'Apocalyptic literature speaks not of the end of *the* world but the ending of 'worlds' plural — our worlds.' And not one of us here will escape the experience, at some time, of feeling that our world, our particular world, or life as we have known it, has ended. In Mark 13, Jesus reminds us that all things will have their time but then pass away. But Jesus also finishes by saying (v31): 'Heaven and Earth will pass away but my words will never pass away.'

Jesus calls us to focus on what endures: neither the building nor the garden before us are the end or ultimate expression of the gospel here in Port Adelaide. They are part of a larger cycle and, like everything else, their time will pass. What will endure are Jesus' words and the truth in them. He said, 'A new command I give you: Love one another. As I have loved you, so you must love one another' (John 13:34)

Love one another: embodied love (love in person and in action), sacrificial love (love concerned with the needs and interests of others) and reconciling love (love that seeks to reach out and overcome differences with others).

The lessons from the garden and our history remind us, as a congregation, to focus not on retaining what we have but on what matters and what lasts: Jesus' words and their truth.

I am the historian for our church and have been for some time. It is not an interest shared by Todd. I am reminded of a meeting we held upstairs, where Todd called it a museum — the interior of the church was what he was referring to. He hastily added that he didn't think that about the people that worshipped there. I suppose he meant me. There is a room — unsurprisingly called the history room — that is set aside downstairs with cardboard boxes full of documents, records and other artefacts. We have celebrated a number of anniversaries lately, one being the 150th year anniversary of the congregation in 2018. For that, we were able to curate an exhibition from material in the history room, and conduct tours around the church for visitors. Such things still happen.

This Tuesday, we are expecting a busload of people taking a tour of local places of worship. Apart from our church, they are visiting the Al Khalil mosque, the Gurdwara Guru Nanak Sikh Temple, and the Phap Hoa Buddhist temple which are all in the western area. It peeves me to have to attend a specialist appointment that day. I have had to arrange for others at our church to welcome them, provide afternoon tea and say some words about Port Adelaide Uniting Church and the Bent Pine Community Garden.

As I mentioned before, our church is a heritage listed building. It requires attention and maintenance at times which cannot be done in any piecemeal or haphazard manner. It all has to be carried out according to strict specifications. It's not that many years ago we had the pipe organ renovated and repainted, along with the decorative frescoes on the interior walls of the church. It really freshened the place up. However, we haven't been able to worship upstairs since COVID-19 arrived. There is another group which now uses our church to worship — they had to move on from where they were because of a redevelopment of the building they used, a not unusual story now. They are a congregation largely made up of people of African origin. They are quite Pentecostal, in contrast to us. But no matter. We get along, although there was an issue recently. One of our congregation members put up a sign on the front noticeboard — the kind that people are meant to read as they walk or drive past. It said, 'Trans kids are welcome here.' This related to a debate that was occurring in our Federal Parliament at the time. We liked it — the sign — but it made members of the other congregation uncomfortable. We are still working on how to resolve such differences.

The other congregation pays us a modest rent. We believe that it is also good stewardship to share what we have and make better use of the building. The upshot of this is that, during COVID, when cleaning became an issue and a burdensome task, it was decided that they would use the sanctuary upstairs and we would worship in the hall downstairs. We start at 9 am and they begin to arrive for their worship upstairs around 10 am. I still miss worshipping upstairs in the sanctuary, but I have moved on as the circumstances have required.

The other recent change to our worship pattern has been, as for so many others, the use of Zoom with its 'mute' and 'unmute' buttons. I make use of this on those occasions when I don't quite manage to get ready in time to be picked up for church.

Todd and I also corresponded between his visits, sometimes by email for shorter messages and sometimes via letter, as a Word document attached to an email. Essentially, the longer letters were Todd's reflections on our conversations, with responses that either hadn't occurred to him on the day or that he might not have felt comfortable putting to me in conversation. The sending and receiving of letters was very familiar to me. Giving these letters due attention, I printed them out and made handwritten notes. I suppose that Todd felt that he could express himself more clearly in the more measured environment of the written page. Mostly, he was right about that. But not always.

In one letter, Todd described my interest in curating the church's history before going on to suggest that the church looks back in abundance but spends far less time looking forward. I thought, 'Well, even though I do the history, I still think the church has got to change.' I read what he wrote as saying that I felt that the church didn't need to change and that I wanted to keep it like it was. The next time we met, I took issue with what he had written.

'This reads, Todd, like I am more interested in keeping things as they are and that you are the one looking forward. And I think that's not quite right. I don't want that. I want the church to change to be more with the community. And to me, that's what the Bent Pine is saying. I understand that the church can't continue as it is because it's got to be more with the community. That's why I think that the CK

Community Hub and the Junction Centre, and what they do at each place, is the church being active.'

Todd was attentive before responding, 'I agree. I accept what you are saying, Ruth. What I have done there is a lazy way of trying to explain the differences between us.

'I think it is fair to say that you have grown up in the Church and it has provided fellowship and a guiding light for pretty much most of your life. I did not grow up in the Church. My parents sent my brother and me to a church school in Sydney. It was an expensive private school. They did it with good motives, to provide us with opportunity. They also did this at some sacrifice financially. However, this experience inoculated my brother against Christianity for the rest of his life. And me, I suppose that I received a partial inoculation. It was the hypocrisy that did it. We saw that faith was well and truly submerged beneath the prestige and profile of the school. Ultimately, the school's values weren't gospel values.'

It seemed like Todd had to get something off his chest. I let him continue:

'Ruth, when my mum got to her late eighties, she became frail. She had macular degeneration and was blind. One Christmas Eve, my brother picked her up from her aged care facility and took her to a carols service at the local Anglican church. Mum remarked some time after, with her humour as healthy as ever, "It made me realise how much Paul loved me. He not only took me to the service but he sat through it with me!" When I next saw him, I complimented my brother on doing that.

He answered, "Yeah, I didn't mind taking Mum, but it was like I'd gotten in some time machine and gone back forty years. Nothing had changed."

'I agree with my brother, Ruth, that going to church is sometimes like being in a museum. It does not surprise me, therefore, that fewer and fewer people choose to go to the same museum every Sunday.'

I replied, 'But it's all about the people. At least it is in our congregation.'

'I don't have any argument with that,' Todd said. 'But you can't get away from the fact that the local church is on a kind of continuum with the wider church. The church, as a local community, can be a great force for good as people contribute to the life and wellbeing of their neighbourhood. The wider church, hovering above the local church, creates the grander narratives about what we, and others, should value and do. We are now in the territory of religion. There is a saying that "Religion is like a finger pointing at the moon." It means that it is God (symbolised by the moon) we should focus on, and not religion itself. It seems to me, however, that religion, as "the finger" has often turned from pointing at God to pointing at its adherents.

'I recently read, Ruth, about a priest in Arizona who had been baptising children with the words "*We* baptise you in the name of Jesus" instead of "*I* baptise you in the name

…". It came to the attention of his Bishop that he had been using these words. Apparently, this was doctrinally wrong since it is supposedly Christ alone, and not the community, who baptises. The result of the priest's error was that all the baptisms he had conducted were declared null and void. Despite being an otherwise exemplary priest, nobody appeared to have any other criticisms of him, he was encouraged to resign.

'The utter hypocrisy. The church was quick to jump on this priest for a semantic error and yet, for so long it has been quite willing to cover up the sexual abuse of children by many other priests (not just Catholic) all over the world.

'Don't get me wrong, Ruth. None of us is immune from being hypocritical. But the church's hypocrisy matters when it positions itself between me and God, with its doctrines and demands. It is then more like an eclipse than it is a pointing finger. It blocks out the moonlight.'

'Well, Todd, what I am interested in is the gathering together of a group of people who care about each other, support each other, and want to make a difference in the world — whether that be on our own doorstep or further afield.'

There were contrasts between Todd and me in our backgrounds and ages — I am just a handful of years younger than his mother — and I accepted that these influenced our respective views of the church. I also accepted his statement that it was not his intention to oversimplify the differences between us (even though he had).

I pressed him, 'Can I ask, Todd, why did you become a Christian when your brother obviously decided not to? I suppose I ask this because you do not seem to have *any* fondness for the church.'

Todd replied, 'Fair question, Ruth. When we moved over to Adelaide from Sydney in the early '70s, my parents seemed to re-evaluate their lives. They had been extremely busy there, both working full time and bringing up three kids. One Sunday night, my mum announced that she felt like going to church. Dad had an Anglican background, and Mum, a Methodist one. They had not been to church for some years. This particular Sunday night, Mum went off by herself. She came back in an elevated kind of mood — maybe, something like your mum did after the Salvos' tent rally. The next Sunday, Dad went. Then they kept going. In all of this, Mum and Dad began talking. What I mean is, communicating, I guess.

'I watched them both for a while. I was around nineteen going on twenty. At that age, children often see their parents as a kind of furniture: that is, part of the place, and needing to be stepped around most of the time, but still occasionally useful as a means of support. Something like that, anyway. Things seemed to change in the house. Mum and Dad began to talk about themselves and their lives, and they did this with an openness I had not seen before.

'One time I was alone with my dad. I told him in conversation what I hated about him. (Yeah, pretty nice of me,

I know.) But this wasn't said in the heat of an argument. It seemed to just well up in me, partly because of the new environment in the house, I think. Anyway, I told him that I hated his shyness and his passivity. (Of course, it was also what I most hated about myself.)

'Dad's response has never left me. He said, using my childhood nickname, "Chunk, I have tried to pull myself up by my bootlaces and change myself, all my life. I realise now that I can't do it. I just can't. But I can now accept myself as worthwhile, just as I am. I have discovered *grace* — undeserved love."

'Ruth, there must be a word for when the meaning of something is conveyed more powerfully by the way a person goes about it, than in the actual words they use to define it. Dad was talking about grace but he responded to me with grace. Not offended, not defensive, not even angry. Instead, there was humility and grace.

'Around that time, I recall sitting in the kitchen with Mum. It was a very small kitchen and we two were sitting around the kitchen table. The table was necessarily small because of the size of the kitchen. It was also circular, like one of those decorative white-painted, wrought iron tables that you see in the shady corners of some gardens. I was apprehensive. I told Mum that I had to go to Sydney. Then I told her the reason. My girlfriend, Karen, with whom I had been trying to maintain an intercity relationship between Sydney and Adelaide, had just let me know that she had missed her period and thought she was pregnant. I was just shy of twenty and she, eighteen. I braced myself for the response. Again, I was surprised by what came. Mum and I had had our share of high-volume fights over the years — she once stopped the car and made me walk home when we were living in the Blue Mountains. Another time after a visit, she had been white-hot furious to find Karen's knickers lost in the sheets at the bottom of my bed.

'Well, there was no heated confrontation in the kitchen that morning. Nor were there accusations regarding my stupidity or other such I-told-you-so's. She said something along the lines of, "You're doing the right thing to go over. But doing the right thing doesn't mean that you have to marry Karen. We're here for you, mate."

'I did go to Sydney, wondering how it was all going to work out. Karen wasn't pregnant. It was another nine months, a troubled gestation period of another sort, before we figured out that our relationship wasn't going to work. But I had been fortified by my mother that day, in that conversation, at that small table.

'Whenever people found faith or religion, it had always appeared (to me at least), that they got louder, more rigid and more prescriptive about what was right and what was wrong. Mum and Dad seemed to go the other way: they got softer, more receptive and … how to put it … they just got more gracious.

'Whatever I think about the church, Ruth, and whatever else has changed for me belief-wise over time, I will never forget my mum and dad and their unscripted lessons in grace.'

CHAPTER TEN

# Wimereux, France 1916 — Poem from the Trenches

By the time we next met, Todd and I had well and truly got past our contretemps. I kept on with my stories.

'I think my oldest brother Reg didn't have a lot to do with Dad but my brother Trev did, I'm sure. Because when Trev died, his son had a box of treasures which Trev had kept, and he loaned it to me so I could make a copy. He also gave me my dad's Bible. He thought I would like that. I think Trev must have had quite a bit of contact with Dad because Dad passed these treasures on to him. Dad and Trev were much more compatible than Dad and Reg. Reg copped a lot of beatings from Dad for doing the wrong thing. I think that he could never quite forgive Dad for that.

'Here, let me show you this "box of treasures". It's just a tin box with a lid. It's not much bigger than a small cake tin.'

Todd began to leaf through its contents. 'Your father certainly kept some interesting mementos of his time during World War I. It shows that he enlisted on 4$^{th}$ April 1916. He was twenty years old. There's a heading, "Trade or calling," for which he has put down, "Labourer."'

'Yes, the two brothers, Dad and Uncle Harry, enlisted on the same day.'

Todd scanned the hundred-year-old papers, 'Here's another document called, "Statement of Service". It reports your father as "Sick to Hospital" on 15$^{th}$ October 1916. By the look of it, it was not long after his arrival in England. He had influenza. It appears that he rejoined his unit, just a couple of days later, on 17$^{th}$ October. He was shipped to France on 25$^{th}$ November with the 43$^{rd}$ Battalion and served on the Western Front.'

'Both boys did.'

'Less than three months later,' Todd went on, 'he was wounded in action on 14$^{th}$ February 1917. "Shrapnel wounds (severe)," it reads. He was admitted to 14$^{th}$ General Hospital at Wimereux before being transferred back to England on 22$^{nd}$ February with "G.S.W. shoulder, arm, wrist". I presume G.S.W. stands for gunshot wound.'

'I believe that while Dad and Uncle Harry weren't in the same sections, they were nevertheless wounded at around the same time, and that a friend of theirs was killed right beside one of them. I remember that Dad had a piece of shrapnel in his wrist that he used to let us kids wriggle around.

The boys always wanted to do it. Not so much us girls. Mum said that he had terrible scars on his back. We never saw those.'

'From there it seems that he was admitted to Northampton War Hospital. Here are some pictures and postcards too. Here's a photograph of some soldiers. The one on the end — Ruth, would that be your dad?'

'Yes, he has a sling on the right arm. That's Dad.'

'He was quite a handsome young man, wasn't he? And judging by the smiles of the nurses, personable too.'

I had to agree! 'You said in your recent letter, Todd, that you didn't think that he was a womaniser. I am not sure that he wasn't … a bit. Apparently, he had a thing with one of the nurses in England, and then he took up with Bonnie back here. So, I think he rather liked women.

'Yes, I did write that. But without wanting to sound certain about it.'

'If you look at the letters in front of you, Todd, it is obvious that one of the nurses was very fond of him. She writes, "I'm missing you and will be glad when you get back." She signs off as "his little sister". It must have been a pet name given by him.

'Oh, I can remember Jenny Fleming once telling me that she burned all George's letters to her, and the family said, "Why did you do that?" Jenny responded, "I couldn't let people see what George had said to me!" I couldn't burn William's, but I don't think that there was anything in those that would cause anyone to turn their eyes upwards.' We laughed.

'I see what you mean.' Todd examined the old postcard in front of him. '"Yours sincerely, your little nurse." There are a lot of photographs. So, these four gentlemen —'

'That's my grandfather — Dad's father — and the three sons from the second marriage. He had three sons from the first marriage too. Dad was from the first marriage. His mum died when they were quite young.'

Todd had shifted back to reading an Australian Imperial Force document. 'It says here, "Return to Australia on 16th September 1917. Discharged 23rd November 1917". After that, your father was granted a pension of two pound five shillings per fortnight.'

'I had his war medals. He had three medals his grandson had put into a little folder. He left it with me but I suggested that he take them back. If anything happened to me then people wouldn't know and I didn't want them to go astray. I still have his Bible.'

Todd picked up some more photographs, swapping their position in his hands, inspecting them like they were playing cards. I provided commentary. There was Mum wringing clothes on wash day on the *Inverlass*. Others of the family in the Hills with the Morton family or at Brentwood on the Peninsula. Another of Trev on his 90th birthday, taken not long before he died in 2014. And then we came to the poem.

# WIMEREUX, FRANCE 1916 — POEM FROM THE TRENCHES

Todd suddenly changed gear, 'Is it personal? Would I be able to read it?'

'Of course! I don't want you to think that you have to read everything. You're welcome to read anything at all.'

He read. 'It says, "To my sister Ruth. Re-written by my father H.S. Fewster, in 1916". The poem is also entitled "To my sister."'

'Dad copied it from somewhere because it was written in 1853. It's not something he wrote.'

Todd read silently. I interrupted the silence, 'To be honest with you, I don't think that I've ever read it.'

'It's interesting', replied Todd. 'It's written by someone who was obviously the black sheep of the family. It's really very self-deprecating. It says:

> *They say I have belied my blood*
> *And stained my pedigree*

He stopped, scanned further lines and then continued:

> *I once had talents fit to win*
> *Success in life's career,*
> *And if I chose a part of sin,*
> *My choice has cost me dear.*
>
> *But those who brand me with disgrace*
> *Will scarcely dare to say*
> *They spoke the taunt before my face,*
> *And went unscathed away.*'

I interrupted Todd, 'You know this is interesting, isn't it? Dad thought that poem was significant. He copied it because that's how he felt.'

'I think so.'

'I don't know why I've never read it. I suppose because it was long, I just sort of put it away and thought, I'll read that later. But that's very significant that it's written in that vein *and* that my father copied it out in full. It's not a short poem.'

'It obviously meant something to your dad.'

'Somebody has written to his sister and Trev thought it was significant to leave it to me. He has also inscribed it "To my sister." I must read it.'

'Here's another verse:

> *With adverse fate we best can cope*
> *When all we prize has fled;*
> *And where there's little left to hope,*
> *There's little left to dread!*'

'Oh really! And he's written it all out longhand on Army paper, so he must have done it during the war, mustn't he?'

'Listen to this verse, Ruth:

> *Sister farewell*
> *Farewell once more to every youthful tie*
> *Friends, parents, kinsmen, native shore*
> *To each and all goodbye*

## WIMEREUX, FRANCE 1916 — POEM FROM THE TRENCHES

> *And thoughts which for the moment*
> *Seem to bind me with a spell*
> *Ambitious hope, loves boyish dream*
> *To you a last farewell.*

'Trev wanted me to have that. He's written on it, "I have thought of you so much. Love Trev." That's from my brother to me.'

'It raises the question of whether Trev gave it to you, just out of your relationship.'

'Yes, he's given it to me because he went through a time where he … you'll recall that I told you that Mum had Dad's grave dug bigger in case Trev did not have anywhere to be buried. He was a bit of a lad. He got into trouble all over the place. He wasn't really a black sheep but he needed a lot of loving.'

'I wonder if Trev and your dad were similar in disposition?'

'Oh, very much so. And I am now thinking, too, that the War had a marked effect on Dad.'

'Yes, at that age — twenty — you normally wouldn't have your hopes and dreams snuffed out, so to speak. It's several pages long, and he has neatly copied the whole thing. You'd have to think he didn't just do it on a —'

'Something to fill in the time. It could have been just after he was injured. It wasn't terribly far into his … It was only two hundred and something odd days. It's not even a year.'

'You can see an awful lot in eight months,' Todd said in a manner that suggested it was a personal observation.

'Oh dreadful! It must affect people when they see friends being killed around them and seeing them lie there. It must affect you.'

'I know from my experience … not being a soldier, but being a health worker in Afghanistan for four years. I was removed from the actual fighting but I was seeing wounded people in front of me and it did take a toll.

'When I hear you talk, Ruth, about the family leaving Lilac Farm on the Peninsula and not coming down to Adelaide once as a family, but instead going back and forth between there and the Peninsula several times chasing work, it reinforces the unsettledness of your dad. It was made worse by not being able to find ongoing solid work. His coming home from the war and his re-adjustment must not have been an easy thing for anyone.'

'Then to be on a ship with four kids that had to be looked after. I must have been a real worry to Mum. You think about trying to learn to walk on a ship. She probably thought, "I did a good job up until that last day." (I laughed.)

'There were two stories about that. Mum was always sure that I slipped on the deck because apparently it was raining, but the boys were sure that I was trying to jump over the openings like they were, but I didn't make it because my legs weren't long enough. I'm not sure which one was right, probably both of them a bit. Life changes you, doesn't it? Experiences you have must change you.'

'Yes, they do. Eva and I were just young — in our late twenties — and to live in a country like Afghanistan and see the suffering ... I was a mess when we came back. It took quite a while, some years really, just to make sense of it all. So yes, we do get changed by what happens to us, and sometimes those scars just stay and become very disabling, and other times, people manage to carry those realities but still turn their life into a positive.

'Ruth, I think maybe your dad, neither trained nor formally skilled, found it hard to find work and succeed and settle in his place.'

'I'd love you to read Reg's little book. It's his memories as a young boy of growing up on the farm on the Peninsula. It describes the early days when Dad and Mum were still trying to make a go of it. I asked him to write his memories down after Mum died.'

'Thank you, Ruth. I would really like to read it. You know, if I wrote your story, I think it would be framed in terms of you and your dad having another opportunity to have that lunch together when you were nineteen. But this time, you could ask each other what you each really wanted to know.'

'I am still unsure about Evelyn's children and how they would feel about all this coming out ... Oh, I think you should just go ahead with it!'

'No, Ruth. I would encourage you to check it out with Kaye and Ken. I get the feeling that this is what you would prefer to do.'

CHAPTER ELEVEN

# Yorke Peninsula 1923 — Lilac and Rocks

We met some two months later and continued our talks about my life. Todd had been reading Reg's little book and wanted to talk to me about it. It was after Christmas. In that time, I had had a pacemaker inserted. There was to be a week of convalescence after this. They said that I needed to not be alone — perhaps they thought something might happen. But where I should stay was the issue.

'As you know, Mike and Jeanette kindly offered to have me in their spare room. We were working out meal times and other housekeeping, and I let them know that I watched *Home and Away* at 7 pm every night. They suggested that I have my dinner in my room (laughter).

'I've got some bad news, I'm afraid, Todd. It's about Evelyn's children and the book. I spoke to Kaye and she said, "Well, it can't hurt Mum now, can it?" But Ken, he lives in the UK, was dead against it: "Mum suffered enough during her life. I don't want her life to be defined by her background as you are doing here."

'I wrote back to him, protesting that I would never say or allow anything to be said about Evelyn that would harm her memory. I loved Evelyn. I thought he would have known me better than that. You might just have to write my story after I'm gone. I won't get into any arguments then.'

'Look, Ruth, I will accept whatever you decide, whether you want to go ahead with it or not.

'Anyway, I wanted to say how much I enjoyed reading Reg's account of his early life. It reminded me of something I read a long time ago. It was a memoir by a West Australian man, Albert Facey. He wrote about his experiences growing up in rural Western Australia in the early part of last century. Like your dad, Bert Facey served in the First World War. To my mind, Reg writes in a similar way about his experiences on the farm and finding his way. I found it equally compelling. His first entry refers to when he was four years old on Lilac Farm. He and Evelyn were playing. He slipped over and cut his arm on a broken bottle at the back of the old wash house. That must have been around 1923.'

'Oh good. I thought you'd like it. You know the land that Dad bought as part of the Soldiers' Resettlement Scheme wasn't much good. Too many rocks. Some farmers were able to buy quite rich land because they had finance behind them. Others had to put up with the farms that really weren't very productive. And Dad had one of those because Mum and Dad used to pick stones all day to clear enough soil to be able to plant. I think the scheme was well-intended but the architects of it didn't think it through very well.'

'I read that when your father first bought the farm, only about 40 acres were cleared for cropping. Altogether they had 990 acres. When your mum and dad left the farm, approximately 500 acres had been cleared. That, plus other memories which Reg wrote down, tells me how hard they worked.'

'Yes, they did. And it must have been very difficult for Dad to do heavy farm work, handling animals and equipment, when the fingers on one of your hands don't work properly. Reg wrote that our mother used to help Father cut the young mallee trees that regrew each year in the paddocks. The children used to go out with them and play around while they worked. It was called Lilac Farm because of all the wild lilac that grew around the place. Grandfather had a bullock team and this was used to clear Mum and Dad's land.'

'Yes, I read that he had a team of sixteen bullocks.'

'Apparently, Mum used to milk thirteen cows each morning and night. But even the children — I wasn't around yet — had to join in. Father had a beautiful team of draught horses, twelve to fifteen of them. Two were "riding horses". Both Mum and Dad were expert riders.'

'There are quite a few stories about horses told by Reg.'

'Yes, apparently one day my father had to shoot one of his favourite saddle horses as, when he let it go after riding it, it rushed down to the water trough, hitting a tree on the way, breaking its leg.

'He also had a stallion called Ben, and unless a mare was in season, Ben worked alongside the others as calm as could be. But if a mare was in season, my father would have to leave this one home, or pandemonium would prevail.

'Reading Reg's accounts reinforced to me, Ruth, just how much horses were part of life for them. I came across these which showed how living and working with horses was part of the children's lives. Can I read you some passages? I do realise that you have read them before.'

I was happy for Todd to read. Listening sometimes gives another perspective on things.

Todd began to 'speak' Reg's words.

> We had one white mare. She used to help load the wagon when the harvest was finished and the grain had to go to market. The method used was to hitch her to the bottom of a bag lifter. I then led her forward — remember I was only seven. The bag would rise and father would take it off and stack it in its place on the wagon. I would then back up the mare until the bag lifter was down on the ground. In those days, bags of grain would weigh 180 pounds. To save him climbing up and down on the wagon,

my father, when he worked alone, would place six bags (one at a time) on the wagon and then go up and stack them.

When we became old enough (about seven years for me) we drove an old mare to school. Auntie Ada helped us to learn to drive our horse to school until we were okay. The mare was an old skewbald (red and white patches). She was called Skewy for obvious reasons. Skewy was a very quiet animal and would put her head down when I went to catch her to allow me to place the blinkers or head stall on her head. She was about 16 hands high, a medium draft mare. This would continue each morning as she was kept in a five acre paddock at the front of our house.

I used to ride her around bareback. She would allow me to pass under her stomach to harness her for school. At the Corny Point Primary School there were only eight children in various classes all taught by the same teacher. Most of the children were related in some way. I remember when I started my uncle George, my auntie Stella, and my auntie Grace all attended. George was about eight years older than me, Stella was about five years older than me. Auntie Grace was about one year younger than me.

Some days during winter, the road through the swamp would be flooded. We drove about five miles to school. About half a mile was through a swamp.

After heavy rain, some days we would have to let our mare carefully pick her way through the water dragging our buggy with her. I remember when the water was two to three feet, it would take us almost half an hour extra time to allow her to transport us through the water without slipping down. On these days we would be very frightened as my father told me if we hurried our horse through this section she could slip and be drowned.

'Oh Todd, to listen to my brother again, and such a world away from Port Adelaide. It was a hard life, wasn't it?'

'Yes, it certainly was, Ruth. But it was salient, for me at least, to be reminded that the family had times of fun. Let me read some more.'

Dad and Uncle Harry made a tennis court at the side of our house and at various times some of our neighbours and the school teachers would come to play. I remember one winter we had so much rain it was two feet deep on the tennis court. Right up under the window of the spare bed room. As most farm kids did in those days, Evelyn and I had made ourselves a brush house or playhouse, down under the trees by the garden. My brother Trevor was too young to play with us, he was only a baby. We spent weeks cutting and carting brush from out of the nearby scrub to build our house. Every farm kid had one — many hours were spent in this one. My uncle Barry (Mum's brother) gave me a couple of homeless lambs which I raised with the help of my parents. When they grew to full size I had trained them to pull a small cart around with me inside it.

My sister Evelyn had a doll's pram. I didn't have a trolley. I earned myself quite a hiding from my father because by removing the cane top of her doll's pram I made a beaut trolley. This happened before we started to go to school.

'That shows how Dad didn't favour one child over the other. Evelyn was always treated equally,' I said conclusively.

'Yes, your father didn't discriminate. Now, Ruth, here's a section that I particularly wanted to talk to you about. I'll read it first.'

Occasionally our uncle Harry who lived with us some of the time would bring his friends the Browns (Darrell, father, Bonnie, mother, and their kids, Ronald, Mavis and Marjory) down to see us and for a couple of weeks we would all join together and roam all over our farm like kids do. We would romp in the hay barns and a thoroughly good time was had by all. One time when they went home they left us a few bottles of soft drink but as my mother didn't find it for a couple of weeks she wasn't sure if it had gone bad. So not wanting to poison her children she emptied it out on the ground — amidst much lamenting from said children.

'When I first read this, Ruth, I realised that in the various references to Harry and Bonnie and your father in our discussions, there's no mention of any kids in that living situation. I am thinking if Harry and Bonnie had taken up after Darrell had died, you would have heard something of the kids in that relationship. But there's no sense of there being kids anywhere in sight. The conclusion I come to is that maybe Bonnie left Darrell and took up with Harry. At that point, the Brown's kids would have still been fairly young, and I can only think, therefore, that they were with their father. And I can see how they would have been pretty frowned upon, Harry and Bonnie, if Bonnie had left her husband and children.'

'Yes, that's right, Todd. If Bonnie had left the children and went with Harry ... I mean we always thought that it was probably Dad — Bonnie became involved with Dad —but it might have been just the fact that Dad was there, and Harry and Bonnie got together. And when Dad needed a home to go to, he went and stayed with them.'

'That's how I read it.'

I tried to make sense of this information as I spoke, 'From their past, Dad would have been friends with the Browns and their children. I'm not sure at what point Uncle Harry and Bonnie would have taken up together. But when

Dad first went back there, if Bonnie and Darrell were together, he may have just been offered a place to stay. Or they — Dad and Bonnie — might still have become a little bit involved. Or maybe she may have left her marriage for Dad. There's no way of knowing any of that.'

'That's true,' said Todd. 'There appears to be no way of verifying any of this. I was talking with Joyce the other day. There was a group of us from church at the local pub the other night celebrating someone's birthday. As you know, she and Greg have recently moved to Perth to be with their family and, more especially, their grandchildren. Joyce was telling me about all the "packing up" jobs that lay ahead of them. In that context, she mentioned that for the last eleven to twelve years, her sister has lived with them. When they were about to move to Perth, Joyce said to her, "What do you intend to do? You can stay in Adelaide or you can come with us."

'Interestingly, despite having an adult daughter in Adelaide, she elected to move with Joyce and Greg to Perth. Hearing that, I realised that *threesomes* aren't always what they appear to be.'

'Dad would have been pretty lonely,' I conceded.

Todd continued, 'Reg had written that Harry "lived with us some of the time." It sounds like Harry was also an unsettled individual if he had that kind of time to just come down and live with his brother and his family. He can't really have had anything more than seasonal work, nothing at least that kept him in a particular place.

'I came across something in *Trove*, the government website, which you may not have heard about, Ruth. It concerns Harry. Certainly, the details of name and date enable the person described in this prosecution to be your Uncle Harry.'

The News *Monday 4th July, 1938*

*Car Attendant's Lapse*

*After the prosecutor had described a car park attendant's lapse as "a mean, despicable offence", Harry Oliver Fewster, of Thornbury street, Kensington Park, was fined £3 with 10/costs, by Messrs. F. Duxbury and J. W.Kennealy in the Norwood Police Court today.*

*The defendant had pleaded guilty to having, at Dulwich, on June 25, been unlawfully in possession of a steel shaft valued at £5, and a slush lamp. Mr. Duxbury, J.P., said that if there had been any previous convictions the defendant would not have had the option of paying a fine. He could consider himself very lucky because of the penalty imposed.*

*Sgt. Bourke, who prosecuted, said that Fewster had not only taken the articles from a place where he was paid £3 a week to prevent pilfering, but he had thrown them later on the premises of an innocent man. The defendant had been employed by the Western Car Park,*

*Victoria Street, Adelaide as an attendant and caretaker, said the sergeant. Fewster had thrown the goods in the man's yard. Had the man discovering them not reported the matter to the police immediately, there might have been an unpleasant stigma against his name.*

*Questioned by the police yesterday afternoon the defendant, at first, denied that he had been in possession of the articles, continued Sgt. Bourke. Subsequently, he had admitted having taken the shaft from a carrier's stand in the car park, thinking it would be useful to him at his home. He had also taken the lamp.*

'Ruth, I can't think that this could be anyone else other than your Uncle Harry.'

'Definitely possible! From what I have heard and know about Uncle Harry, definitely possible!'

'So not only did your father Bert have trouble settling back into life at home, Harry, it seems, did, too, and got into trouble with the law. Since we looked at the box of treasures last time, I was able to find out one new thing and reflect on another, concerning your dad and his brother in World War I. The first was that on Harry's World War I service record, it is reported that he was gassed in the trenches in France. It happened in May of 1918. So, putting it all together, Harry was dangerously ill with influenza in England before he even saw action. This was August 1916. Then in February 1917, at a similar time to Bert, he suffered a gunshot wound to the left arm that was classified as severe. And was hospitalised once more. He was barely twenty years of age. Then, in the year after that —1918 — he was sent back to the Front and was gassed in the trenches.'

'What the war must have done to these young men!'

Todd continued, 'One of the other things we talked about last time, Ruth, was how it appeared that Bert was a bit of a ladies' man. Since then, I have been able to listen once more to the recording of our meeting. At that meeting, I had read aloud part of a letter from one of the nurses that Bert had befriended. I listened to it again and wrote it down. I'll read it to you. In this letter, she makes reference to the inclusion of a picture of her brother even though I don't recall seeing that picture in the box of treasures. She grieves her brother:

*who was such a beautiful boy. I cannot tell anyone what a loss has gone out of my life by losing Fred. And yet, Bert, it is a relief to know that he is out of all the pains and sufferings of war. You boys are all so very brave. So we who are left at home must be brave. It is a woman's war as well as a man's. May came home yesterday. She does miss you boys. You were such good friends to her. I'm sure the girls would send their love.*

'Dad kept all these letters. They meant something.' (Keeping things. It was one of the first times that I could see a shared disposition between my father and me.)

'Yes, they did mean something,' said Todd. 'The correspondence is very heartfelt. Bert was obviously a bit of a goer with the girls. But I also see in these exchanges young people experiencing traumatic and life-changing events and finding a camaraderie to help each get through them. I see flirtations but no direct romance.

'And, one more thing, Ruth, there was a letter from Harry to Bert that caught my eye. Bert had been repatriated back to Australia by this time. Harry's letter had the expected chitchat from one brother to another. But it also let Bert know that a cable would be coming in the next day or so asking for money to be sent. It made me smile a bit, as I am sure that this was a request played out more than once over the years from the younger to the elder brother.'

I was being offered perspectives about my father and his life that had never been offered to me before. William had, for so many years, been my greatest support, but with respect to my father, William did just that: supported my views rather than question them. I guess that he saw what had happened to the family, and that was enough for him. He made his conclusions about Dad and that, in turn, further cemented mine. I'm not being hard on William for it. He just knew how hard it was for us, and his view was coloured by my reaction to the lunch. He couldn't have seen it any other way.

Coming across that hand-copied poem, though, opened my thinking to just who Dad might have been rather than the person I had framed in my mental picture of him all these years. I resolved to ask Todd at church on the weekend whether it might be possible sometime to re-visit that lunch with my father. He had described it as an opportunity last time we spoke. I was now thinking that I would like to take that opportunity.

CHAPTER TWELVE

# Port Adelaide 1949 — 'The Dinner' Revisited

'So, Ruth, you got my email this week outlining an approach to how we might look back at that dinner. I decided to structure it as a series of questions which you weren't able to ask then but do ask here, together with your father's answers. Of course, what we're doing is a reconstruction. It's not meant to be "this is what happened."'

'It's imagining what could have happened and how different the outcomes could have been. I get that.'

'Yes, just an opening up of possible interpretations about how things were, given, it seems to me at least, that nobody really knows what happened between your mum and your dad.'

'No, no.'

'And that'll be how it stays, I reckon ... By the way, before we start, I was looking in *Trove* and found out that your grandfather Walter passed away in Yorketown Hospital in 1951. I'm thinking that's possibly when your dad moved down to Dudley Park and got the deli.'

'Yes, that's probably right. When his father died, Dad surely inherited something — a portion. Grandfather owned land and farms in 1951. How old would I have been then?'

'You would have been twenty-two. Your dad died in 1966, so he would have had maybe a ten-year working life in the shop before retiring in Blackwood.'

'Three years after that dinner when I was nineteen. That's interesting. I wonder if, in coming back down to Dudley Park, Dad thought he might reconnect with the family. I wouldn't be surprised if that's where Trev had a lot of contact with him — at the shop.'

'Yes, I think that he would have had contact with Trev. And I daresay, when he saw Trev, he got news about you.'

'Oh, he would have.'

'Trev would've told him what Ruth was doing. And that was almost enough for him. It had to be.'

'It had to be. He wouldn't have had any encouragement from me because I wasn't in a state to be kind to that idea. I reckon that's true. That's what would have happened.'

Todd asked me if I would like him to read on.

'Yes, please do.'

As Todd read, he was recreating a conversation with Father that I wish we had had over seventy years ago.

'Why did you leave, Dad?'

'That's a difficult question to answer in any simple way, Ruth. It's complicated. Firstly, I want to acknowledge to you my shortcomings as your father: I have not been a good dad. And yet, my failings were not because of a lack of love for you or of my having little interest in your welfare and life.'

'But you left us when we needed you most!'

'When you were badly injured on the *Inverlass* on that final day, it was like the capstone on another failure on my part to properly protect and care for my family. It followed on from a failure to make a 'go' of the farm — that was a real disappointment. How hard your mother and I worked in that time! Then there was the job at the piggery, then back to Marion Bay on the wharves, then back to the city and Port Adelaide. They were hard times and it was hard to hold on to a good job. I tried my best to get ahead and look after the family — and to be somebody better than I was or, at least, had so far proved to be. I was somewhat of a disappointment to your mother. She was always the stronger one.

'On that day when I carried your almost lifeless body up that rope ladder, fearful of how badly you might be injured, I was numb with worry — and deeply shocked. I had not experienced that kind of fear and stress since the war. Being plunged into that once more was traumatic — maybe, even worse than being injured myself since it was my little girl who lay as a crumpled body at the bottom of the ship.'

'Nevertheless, Dad, you still left us at a time of great need, and we just didn't know why you did that. I have been so angry with you.'

'I can't recall exactly the sequence of events after your accident. We were all terribly upset. Things had been tense between your mother and me for some time. She was naturally very upset over what had happened to you. I suppose we each felt guilty and to blame for what had happened, and we were trying to deal with that in our own ways. I can't remember what we said to each other. And I probably don't want to. Painful memories. I hope that I didn't accuse her of not keeping an eye on you. If so, I regret such a statement. Deep inside, I felt that it was I and not her who had neglected their responsibility to look after the family.

'Once you were in hospital, it seemed best if I started earning a wage once again. So, I went to Warooka. The communication between your mother and me — as well as how we were feeling about each other and the future — became complicated and unclear. I was up there and she was down here in

Adelaide, and it was hard to be "in touch" with each other in any meaningful or helpful way that could help us get through this time.'

'Why were things tense between you and Mum before my accident?'

'I don't think she was very happy about having to move back to the country following the decommissioning of the *Inverlass*. She expressed doubt that serving in Cadd's Emporium was going to be a long-term, secure job and, by extension, provide security for the family. She didn't say much, but I could see she wasn't happy about that and about uprooting everyone once more for an uncertain future.

'It's hard to say why our marriage faltered, Ruth. I was a changed man, as was Harry, when we came back from the war. I went away as something between a boy and a young man and came back as a "damaged" adult. It was not just the injuries to my arm and fingers either. Those made it harder to farm and to work generally than would otherwise have been the case. It was the things I had seen, the sounds I had heard, and the fear and desolation I had experienced in the trenches which most damaged me. How can one explain those things to people when you don't understand them yourself? And how could they understand them anyway if they hadn't been there?

'And Mum, well, she had her baggage too. I did my best to love her and support her but there was something about what happened to her that left her damaged in her thinking about herself too. I suppose that we were two young people trying our best to raise a family and provide for them, but the headwinds of adversity — and memory — buffeted us without let-up and, in the end, blew us and our relationship away.'

I had listened intently but without need for comment up to this point. I suppose I had been reflecting recently on what my father went through in France. And so it just came out, 'That long ago they just didn't realise what it did to those men. It's taken another fifty odd years to realise just how badly it affected people. Nobody wins out of a war.'

Todd joined in, 'They went off as though it was the greatest adventure, especially World War I, and really the trenches were just hell on earth. And then for your father, in succession, to come back, get married and begin farming — alright, there's some hope and a future there — but then the farm doesn't work out.'

'The farm failed.'

Todd continued his synopsis, 'Then he comes down and gets another job in a piggery, and then that — however well or not that went — that finishes, and he's back to the Yorke Peninsula for another job. Then that finishes and he's back down to Adelaide to get the caretaker job, and then running into the Depression at the time of the *Inverlass* … they were tough times.'

'Oh, they were terrible times. Dad was really strong when you think about it. We probably didn't give him enough credit for being strong, but we didn't understand, did we?'

'No, possibly not. But I think your mum was strong. I think your dad resigned himself to failure in some ways: "I don't seem to be able to make a go of much." When you had your accident, I imagine your mum and your dad … it was such a stressful time ... they may not have had kind words for each other at the time.'

'No, I think Mum probably would have torn strips off Dad for leaving the thing open that I fell down.'

'Yes, and he may have thought, "Well, you should have been looking after the young ones!"'

'That's right: "You should have had them inside instead of letting them run around the deck."'

'Yes, and whether those things were said or whether they were just felt, I have a feeling that it was such a traumatic time. It was really tense, and they were then separated for some weeks.'

'Yes, and they didn't have modern phones and things like we do now by which they could contact each other. Dad wasn't earning terribly much and he wasn't able to send much. Some weeks, Mum wouldn't have anything to buy food with. The whole situation was terrible.'

'It was just one of those sad situations. If you think of a young person come back from the war and then, of course, there was what your mum went through …. She had to cope with that terrible experience. So, you put those two young people together and put them in a Depression —'

'And expect smooth sailing with no problems.'

'Shall I read some more, Ruth?'

'Yes, go on.'

Then Todd began to read again, and I was at lunch with my father once more.

> 'I have to ask, Dad. Did you leave Mum for another woman?'
>
> 'No, I did not. I was lonely, no doubt about that. At the time, I needed a place to stay and was able to stay with Harry and Bonnie. It is not easy being someone who is perceived as having abandoned their family. Harry and I, we understood each other. We both understood how hard it was to settle back into life here afterwards. Very few others knew that. But Harry and I could look after each other. And we did.
>
> 'Of course, Harry struggled in his own way to fit into life at home after the war. He and Bonnie were tolerated rather than accepted in the area up there. On the other hand, I felt accepted and less judged living with them. And so, there we were, the three of us — all outsiders in one way or another.

'I did write to you when I could: birthday cards and Christmas greetings. I really did think of you. And, probably not as regularly as it should have been, I tried to send money down to your mother. I wasn't flush with it.'

I interjected before Todd had got very far. I was obviously seeing Dad's perspective more readily now, 'Yes, Dad did send Christmas and birthday cards every year. When he did go to Warooka, I can see that it was a logical thing for him to gravitate toward Harry.' Todd paused for me to make my point before continuing. He picked up the dinner conversation at a point where I was speaking.

'After Evelyn's wedding, we had a lovely time at the "trots". I actually felt some joy at being together: you, me, the boys and the uncles. So why was there such a long silence afterwards? I am talking about six or seven years without seeing you!'

Dad answered me, 'Ruth, this has been one of the hardest things for me to endure as your father, just as it has been for you. I decided to write to Evelyn before her wedding and let her know the truth of her origins. I knew that I would be asked to give her away. I was happy to do that. I also knew for those few hours that we would be "together" — at least in appearance — as a family. And, if that was the case, then I wanted her to know at least some better truth about me: that instead of only being a father who abandoned her, I was instead someone who had voluntarily taken her on and given her a home, a family and care. I thought I had that right. But your mother was absolutely furious when I did this. She let me know that I had jeopardised Evelyn's future — and possibly that of the rest of the family — by revealing this secret. I think she snapped the lid tightly shut on this matter once more, and part of that was to tell me that my interventions weren't welcome. I retreated. And that was also a mistake.'

At that point, as Todd continued to read in the voice of my father, something strange happened. It was as if Dad had excused himself from the dinner table in 1949 and was speaking to me in the present from beyond the grave. I am not sure whether Todd really intended this. He gave no sign of it and kept reading. As Dad was speaking to me, I was reminded of the presence of that mysterious male figure, dressed in white, who appeared at my bedroom door — to comfort me when I was in such distress after William had expressed his unreadiness for marriage.

'And that brings us back to that dinner all those years ago. It was my attempt to see how you were and how your life was going. But it was, I think, for both of us, an awful experience. How could we have said the things to each other that we needed to, when some of what needed to be said was off-limits?

'Then again, perhaps I did not try hard enough, did not persevere sufficiently. I was used to failing at things by then, including accounting for my actions. And if that cemented an impression that I did not care for or have an interest in you, I am so sorry. What I would have really wanted to say to you then was to ask your forgiveness and tell you, as imperfect as it was, that I loved you and was proud of you.

'We moved back to the city sometime after the death of Father in 1951. It enabled me to be closer to the family, at least to the boys – I saw a bit of Trev. It was harder for me to make contact with you, living as you were with your mother, and based on the difficulties of our previous time together. But I felt closer anyway and heard some news.

'I hope that you can forgive me for all those lost years. I believe your mother did forgive me near the end. At least, she offered a kind of reconciliation at the time of my 70$^{th}$ birthday. I was very grateful to her for that. I was so glad to see the family. I died some nine months after that birthday, and Harry passed on some seven months after me: both of us in 1966. It was as if we had cast our lots together, in life and in death.'

I am a person who usually has reasonable control of my emotions. But there was a pause here while I dabbed at my eyes with a hanky. 'Oh Todd! That is such a beautiful way of working through that. It helps me so much to hear how it could have been, and that's a real comfort to me. He really did love me ... and the visit he paid to the Willason's ... I ran to him and jumped into his arms and he really hugged me.'

Todd replied, 'Ruth, questions remain unanswered, regarding your parents' separation and *who* decided *what*: not to go, as in your mum deciding not to take the family to Warooka — or not to come back — as in your father not returning from Warooka or, indeed, telling your mum not to come with the family to Warooka. The *least* likely thing that I think happened, and it is only my opinion, is that Bert went off and straight away fell in love with someone with sufficient passion to forsake his family.'

I agreed. 'I don't think that happened either. In hindsight, I don't think that happened. When I was young, Mum was quite sure that that's what had happened. But she ... I don't think that she could accept the fact, really, that Dad just didn't want to come back to her.'

'And maybe he felt he couldn't measure up, or whatever, to his obligations as husband, father and provider,' suggested Todd.

I thought about this. 'He tried to keep contact with his family. But then Mum asked Evelyn not to write to him. Ken told me that just recently in that letter where he told me I couldn't do this — that is, go ahead with the book. He said straight out, "You don't know how much Mum suffered." And that Ken knew how hard it was for his mother because she was asked not to write to her "father" anymore because it upset Mum too much. Apparently, Evelyn was writing to Dad up to a decent age until Mum got cranky and asked her not to write. And that wasn't nice of Mum, really.'

'I have been wondering, Ruth, whether your mum's experience of being cut off from seeing her grandchildren by Trev's ex-wife, Elaine, and the pain that caused her played a part in changing her mind about re-establishing family contact with your dad. In stopping Evelyn's contact with your dad, she had done something like Elaine had done to her. We don't know whether Bert contacted your mum and let her know that he had a condition which meant that he wouldn't see his 71st birthday. He may have. I also think it quite possible that after your mum's baptism, she examined a lot of things in her own life, and this led to a change of heart.'

I nodded. 'I believe that. I really felt it was Mum's way of recognising that she hadn't forgiven Dad, and this was her way of doing so. We all went and we all had to "chip in" for a watch. It was a reconciliation on her part to put things right before he died.

'Things can change when you know more information and can think your way through things — when you have certain information and can change your concept of things. And that's exactly what happened with Dad. Firstly, with Mum and now with me.

'It's a dreadful thing to say that I was relieved when Dad passed away before I got married. I was angry at him and my not allowing him to give me away at my wedding would have hurt him terribly. But now I feel totally different. And I wouldn't mind having those thoughts — even my dreadful ones — made known.'

# CHAPTER THIRTEEN

# Cheltenham 2021 — The Third Secret

Last weekend Port Adelaide played Gold Coast. Both teams needed to win to make the final eight. Todd told me that he was going to the Adelaide Oval to watch, and that he would message me during the game to provide an 'at the ground perspective', as he put it. It was a close game. Port won by just two points, and the staccato SMS banter was just another conversation in a myriad over the past eighteen months:

End of 1$^{st}$ quarter
Todd: Ruth, so far so good
Ruth: Wow!
End of 2$^{nd}$ quarter
Todd: Not so good that quarter
Mid 4$^{th}$ quarter
Ruth: I am having palpitations

Todd: Stay calm
Ruth: ????
Todd: I know what you mean. I'm not that calm
Ruth: I am shaking
Todd: Too close
Ruth: Yeah, still 9 minutes to go
End of game
Ruth: It couldn't have happened better. I am exhausted
Todd: Sorry for delay. Was walking across the bridge to the station. I'm also exhausted. 😊
Ruth: 😊 😊

It was about this time that I had to have a biopsy on an artery in the temple area of my skull to exclude the condition temporal arteritis. There was the possibility of sudden permanent blindness. Well, I had the test and it was thankfully negative. Nevertheless, I was told that I had to have support for a few days before I could resume living alone. So, it was back to Mike and Jeanette's place.

I told Todd about the fall in the shower while staying there.

'Actually, it was two falls in the shower. Following the first one, Mike got me a plastic chair that was at their community garden near the city. This was so I could shower sitting down. It was a good idea, and I was able sit down and shower myself. The problem was that the chair had been weakened by exposure to the sun over a protracted period. And so, at an unexpected and inopportune moment, it gave way. I suppose it more than gave way. It broke into pieces, several of which seemed to embed themselves underneath me while I lay on my back on the floor in the shower cubicle.

'I was unable to help Mike and Jeanette get me up off the floor. Mike had brought a towel in to cover me while he looked in another direction. This set me off. Giggling, I should say, 'Oh Mike, don't worry about that. There's nothing there that you haven't seen before.'

'Well, with little progress, Mike and Jeanette had to call in two of their neighbours to help. They came into a room that seemed to be filling rapidly. There seemed to be a lot of people in there, even though there were just four apart from me.'

'It gives new meaning to the expression, "open inspection."'

Todd's one-liner reached its audience, and I giggled once more.

'It was hilarious. Here I was handing them pieces of broken plastic chair which I was extricating from my buttocks. I knocked my head and stirred up my shoulder pain, but thankfully I didn't break anything, apart from the chair, of course.

'This kind of episode seems to be happening more and more frequently. And where my week used to be punctuated by a few medically related appointments, now they seem to crowd out my other commitments. It's annoying.'

'I can see it would be, Ruth.'

'Oh well! There it is. That's how it stands. On a brighter note, that busload of people who were doing a tour of local places of worship the other week bought $22 worth of the jam I had made and left at church. That makes it $291 for the year. I think I'll give that to Frontier Services.'

'Well, Eva and I have certainly enjoyed that Satsuma plum jam you gave us. It's the "vehicles" that are required to eat it — yes, slices of bread or toast — that are my problem.'

'Thanks for your email after last Thursday, Todd. I appreciate your concern. Two hours for our talk was a little longer than usual. But no, you didn't tire me out. I enjoy your visits very much. I really appreciate the way you think. You express situations in such a way that really gels with me and, in many ways, helps me to think more clearly about them.'

'Ruth, the letter that came with that email was the second time I've felt a degree of trepidation in writing to you.'

'To be truthful, Todd, when I finished reading the last paragraph, I bawled my eyes out. It made me realise there are things in my shadow I haven't dealt with. And I need to do that. It's probably something I need to do on my own because it's very private and personal. It concerns my relationship with William which was really strong. It went for thirty-five years — it had to be strong, didn't it? There were things that happened that I didn't deal with at the time. I just put them away because it would have caused too much upset if I had tried to address them and change them. I couldn't change them. I learned how to deal with them to a certain extent, but I tucked a lot of them away in my shadow because that was the way I handled it. So, when you presented it like this, it was helpful to me.'

'I'm glad about that, Ruth. I like the paradox that the closer we walk in and approach the light, the greater the shadow we cast. It helps explain "me" to myself.'

'Yes, that is brilliant. I read that as saying that we all have a shadow. It doesn't matter who you are — saint or sinner! I've written a question mark here somewhere in the notes I made. You wrote, "I believe there's one more part of the shadow." Would you take me through what you mean by that?'

'Yes, I was trying to make sense of why Ken would be so against having his mother be part of any story of your life. As you said, he strongly expressed to you that he didn't want his mother to be part of any book. He did not want her to be defined by her origins.

'I am pretty sure that there was ongoing suffering in Evelyn that permeated, one way or another, through to her children. They were very aware of how their mother felt.

'For instance, when she told you in Wesley House that your father was not who you thought he was — in other words, that Bert was not your father, this greatly unnerved you. Reg had to jolt you back to reality. And yet, your unpleasant experience was just an insight into what had occupied Evelyn's soul for so many years.'

'I have to say — and I didn't know this until just a couple of months ago — I went down to visit my niece, Evelyn's daughter Kaye, and I said, "Oh, I cut that cake crooked. That was one thing Evelyn used to do." Kaye replied, "I know. One day we were coming home from Grandma's in the car — *when Mum and I were still living at the back of Reg's place* — and Mum was really angry because Aunty Ruth had told her not to cut the cake crooked."

'So, she was really cross. It had obviously touched something that made her conscious that I was different from her.'

Todd said, 'It's amazing how little acts like that can have tentacles down to deeper things.'

'Absolutely. And I thought about that and I would never have upset her deliberately. After Kaye told me, I said, "Goodness, I had no idea it upset your mother." And Kaye repeated, "On the way home in the car she kept on about it, saying how terrible it was with Ruth going on at her for not cutting the cake straight."'

'I can imagine Evelyn thinking,' said Todd, "My life wasn't even *cut straight* while yours always *was*."

He continued, 'According to Jung, who wrote about all this, we have little awareness of those things that exist in our "shadow". It usually takes someone else to point them out to us. I wonder now whether one of the mechanisms that calls us to confront what is in our shadow may be the unveiling of secrets.'

'Well, that could be right. There's certainly been enough of them in my family.'

'Ruth, when we were speaking some time ago about Reg cutting the top off Evelyn's doll's pram in order to make himself a "beaut trolley"— as he called it — you made the point that there was never any hint of difference in how the children were treated. And yet, and this appears to be the casualty of secrets, Evelyn did acutely feel her difference. And that feeling stayed with her.

'It seemed to confront her every now and again, like when your mum went into care at Wesley House. If Evelyn wanted to take her out for the day, Mabel often didn't have time. But if you wanted to take her out then she was always available. You mentioned to me how Evelyn felt hurt by that. You didn't think there was much in what she was saying but it was Evelyn's felt experience.'

'I didn't realise any of this until Ken said it was the pain she felt. And then you wrote about our shadows. That, to me, was a revelation.'

'Like another secret revealed. My take on Ken's opposition to your story being told, Ruth, hinges on that lack of awareness of Evelyn's suffering. Seeing it from Ken and Kaye's perspective, if this unawareness was to be somehow perpetuated in any account of Aunty Ruth's life, then this would be unbearable as a reminder of their mother's pain

— even if nice, complimentary things were said about their mum.

'I can understand why Ken would want to leave things unspoken but I'd also like to think that if he could hear what we have discussed, he would hear a different story from the one he currently knows.'

CHAPTER FOURTEEN

# The Bent Pine Compost

Todd was weeding thistles that had sprung up between the Jacobean lilies, bromeliads, and fairy lachenalias on the bank beneath four large plane trees. Another resident, a blue tongue lizard, pottered between clumps of greenery, venturing as far as the sole native hollyhock that bordered the old tennis court. Todd looked upwards periodically to relieve his neck from this head-down work and to keep an eye out for his pottering companion.

Across the garden, over the lawn, his eyes panning the stonework of the church, Todd's gaze locked onto a section of gutter just proximal to the corner buttress. It sat some fifteen metres up the vertiginous back wall. The gutter was twisted outwards, ready to pour its received rainwater, like a libation, directly onto the ground below. It was probably caused by a falling branch from one of the plane trees. He had seen it before, and more than once, Todd had suggested to the other gardeners, tongue in cheek, of course, that one of them might like to climb up and fix it.

His church was passing. He knew that. It was partly because the grand old building now pointed its wrought iron finger at an ageing congregation and demanded to be maintained in the style to which it was accustomed. At the same time, the world around it sought new sources of spiritual and moral inspiration, so few, if any, fresh (or youthful) reinforcements would be on their way to save this church.

The church, at large, had its own 'shadow' too. This shadow was not just filled with its past misdeeds, covered up or otherwise. It hid a deeper paradox, well-mortared into its foundations. It was this: the church preached a gospel of letting go of, or dying to, an old life so that new life could come — death followed by resurrection. And yet, it held on tenaciously to its buildings, traditions and programs until non-theological realities took them away regardless.

It was therefore not surprising to Todd that, when faced with the approaching end of something — a group, an entity or a project — some people could allow themselves to accept it while others thought that such acceptance was a premature 'giving up'. There was also a middle, even oscillating position, that he shared at times, which hoped for some unforeseen intervention that might change everything. Not uncommon end-of-life dilemmas, he thought.

Todd could acknowledge the place, even the importance, of institutions in providing values and rules for community order and the common good. The church was one of these institutions. Nevertheless, he believed that when the time did come, despite what it had provided over time for so many people (including his friend Ruth), the church, as it was, could be let go without also jettisoning grace, forgiveness and reconciliation. For him, these were the cornerstones of faith and humanity. Community could still be found.

He scooped up a handful of revitalised soil from the deeper layers of the compost. An anemone of earthworms, balled and pulsating, sat in his upheld palm. They were beautiful, especially for what they signified — healthy earth. But it was not just the worms. It was a cast of thousands. The earwigs, beetles, millipedes, slaters, cockroaches, and these glorious earthworms, an ecological workforce of myriad shapes and functions, all did their thing in the miraculous process of breakdown and regeneration. It was largely carried out without our attention or awareness but, nevertheless, led to the transformation of organic waste into rich, dark soil.

Belief and tradition (and buildings) weren't the only things that could become stale and no longer able to nourish their adherents. Every bit of us, the good, the bad and the ugly, found its way, eventually, into compost to be broken down. The bloom of flowers and the rapacity of weeds — our crowning achievements and our bitter regrets — all had the same status there. To stand by the turned compost, with a fistful of its thrumming soil, was to hold the very exudate of hope. He looked at what was in his hand with the wonderment of a child.

CHAPTER FIFTEEN

# The Book of Ruth

Todd recalled the approach in the previous year by a group from Ruby House. Ruby House is a community mental health program (non-government) that offers its members opportunities to explore friendships, re-establish links with family, and participate in what they term 'work-ordered day activities'. Their meeting place and offices were just down Commercial Road, on the other side of the railway underpass. They were wondering if some of their members might be able to do some gardening at the Bent Pine.

Over the last year and a bit, the friends from Ruby House had really invested in their plot at the Bent Pine. They worked the new raised garden bed where the old hall once stood. They beautified and enhanced this garden plot with 'worm resorts', a bird bath and with discreet laminated signs indicating what herb or plant was growing in a particular place. Lengths of cane had been bound and fashioned into trellises for climbing sweet pea and support of tomato vines, giving further texture and shape to the garden.

While digging the plot, they encountered big chunks of bluestone and red brick which were scattered there following the demolition of the hall. ('There we were thinking that we had dug most of these out,' smiled Todd.) Following an explanation of the rocks' origin, Peter and Richard from Ruby House placed them in a mortar/cement mix within wine barrel hoops and made five large stepping stones. They set them in the ground beside the raised garden bed. It was a gift.

It was garden church. The theme for the day was taken from a Bible story in the Old Testament — the Book of Ruth. A woman called Naomi and her husband have emigrated from Israel with their two sons to the land of Moab. They are originally from Bethlehem in Judah but have left because of famine in the land. While in Moab, Naomi's husband dies. Her two sons married Moabite women, one named Orpah and one named Ruth. After around ten years, both sons die, leaving Naomi and her two daughters-in-law alone and without support.

The activity for garden church that morning in late spring involved *gleaning*. Gleaning was an Old Testament practice, formalised in the law. Gleaning meant that the poor could go to fields that were being harvested and pick up the leftover grain that the landowners were required to leave in the field for that purpose. It helps keep Naomi and her daughter-in-law Ruth alive after they arrive back in Judah where they have no other means of obtaining food.

Today, members of the congregation would glean from the garden any artefact that might give them hope. It could be a flower, plant, vegetable, fruit, or even a weed, which reminded them of beauty not yet extinguished. Or, it might prompt them to further action in caring for a natural world under threat. Gleaning was about gratitude for small things or leftovers.

Todd spoke:

> It is hard to appreciate the vulnerability that the widow Naomi and her daughters-in-law, Ruth and Orpah, face after her sons both die. In such a patriarchal society, there is absolutely no safety net. We still see today, in Afghanistan, widows begging on the side of the road, dangerously adjacent to the passing traffic. If you don't have a husband, sons or other family network, you are in deep trouble. For Naomi, too, following the death of her husband and sons, the persons you would then traditionally rely upon for support (your kith and kin) are not there: she is in a foreign land. She, Ruth and Orpah are literally in danger of starvation.

Naomi's best bet is to travel back to her land of Judah, but there is no obvious future there for her widowed daughters-in-law. It is in this context that Naomi urges Ruth and Orpah to return to their families in Moab. Being widows, they will still have a place, some sort of welcome and therefore some security. We can follow her logic and the narrow set of options: Do you think that I can provide husbands for you in Judah? Even if I could marry and have more sons, will you be able to wait while they grow up so that you can marry them? Of course not! Better that you go home where you have a chance at a future.

Orpah very reluctantly decides to take Naomi's advice and leaves in tears. Ruth refuses to do so. She is determined to stay by Naomi's side. And so, Naomi gives up trying to convince her. It is interesting to read that Ruth does not declare that she is doing this because it is 'the right thing to do' or 'this is what God would want me to do' or anything such like. She does it because she loves Naomi and is committed to her.

Ruth has the option to go back to her past — her family — as a means of getting out of this terrible situation of vulnerability and uncertainty. She chooses not to. Neither does she focus on the future — to do so for her would be paralysing, because, as

Naomi has outlined, there appears to be no future. Ruth remains in the present, focussing on her relationship with and love of Naomi. It is this which guides her. She accompanies Naomi back to Judah and eventually things work out well.

Friends, there are similarities between Ruth's dilemma and ours. As a congregation, we face uncertainty and significant challenges to our ongoing presence here. We probably all agree that we can't go back — back in time when congregations were larger and society was different. And while we have given much thought, individually and collectively, about the future and its options, there is no clear or certain pathway just now — even though decisions will eventually be made. What we can do, however, is to be in the present and, like Ruth, remain committed to each other with both love and respect. It may not seem like a solution but, as it turns out for Naomi and Ruth, it is the basis for the best solution — the best way forward.

When he next met with me, Todd recalled the garden church reflection. He expressed a conviction that, like the friends from Ruby House, I had taken things from the past and transformed them into something new.

'Ruth, when I spoke the other day about Ruth and Naomi and their dilemma of not being able to go back while not knowing the best way forward, I have to confess that I was thinking about how this applied to me personally and not just the congregation. It encapsulated how I have been feeling about my faith and my place in the church.

'The book of Ruth speaks to me from antiquity and you, you, Ruth, have spoken to me, I won't say from your antiquity,' a ripple of laughter paused him, 'but you have spoken to me in the present. In that Old Testament story, you become Naomi for me and I become Ruth. I have been reminded that friendship cuts through any number of issues, theological or otherwise.'

'Thank you, Todd. We each have a different journey but the same faith. I think that truly understanding each other's stories, whatever they may be, is the church at its best.'

'Yes, I agree, Ruth. But sometimes even being able to tell one's story is problematic. Not that long after we returned from Afghanistan in 1987, there was a church camp. It was in the Barossa, I think. At this camp, the leaders spoke about how we each wear masks to establish our various personas (at work and in social situations). They argued, quite rightly, that we should become better at removing our masks and being more honest with each other. I remember getting up and leaving the meeting to walk around the town where the camp had been held. My distress was twofold. I did not know how to remove my mask: it held in everything I had seen and experienced. The other problem was that those around me, including those at church, had not welcomed any attempt on my part to remove it, or even shown any sign that they wanted me to remove it. It seemed the fact we were safely at home should be all that we needed for our mental health. That made me even more frustrated.'

Todd continued, 'About two years ago, I was asked, as were a couple of other members of the congregation, to share an experience of hope. It was Easter Sunday morning, the time of celebrating the risen Jesus. Because of COVID, we were worshipping via Zoom. The gospel reading for the day was from Mark chapter 16. In it, we read of the two Marys' and Salome's encounter with the empty tomb. The emptiness is like an evaporation of their hopes. And in the original manuscripts it is here, as the women leave the empty tomb trembling and bewildered, that the gospel of Mark ends.'

'For some reason I chose to recall a story from Afghanistan, not an obvious topic to engender hope. It was an experience which linked the lives of my father and an elderly Afghan man who had presented at the Red Cross Hospital because of painful knees. I should add that my dad had a massive stroke while Eva and I were in Afghanistan at this time. He died in the hours after it. We were so far away and not able to be with Mum and the family until some days later. It added significantly to my anguish and helps explain why the details of the Afghan man with painful knees will, for me, never pass into vagueness.'

'On this Easter Sunday morning, I started sharing this story with the group online.

He had white hair, thinned and wispy as hair seems to go in advanced age. A single remnant tooth populated his mouth (at least as far as I could tell). It was an incisor, top right. The muscles in the arms, legs and face were wasted, producing a haggardness beyond any fatigue which might have been brought on by travelling here from the countryside. The skin on his legs was friable: it seemed like it would tear as easily as paper, a suspicion heightened further by the unhealed sores down each shin.

I asked my Afghan colleague Sanguin, in Dari, how old this man was. The man heard me and answered himself. I knew immediately that he had understood the import of my question, and I was suddenly embarrassed by it. 'I am fifty-five. I am old before my time,' was what he said, almost guiltily, in a gesture of resignation. I was sorry to have turned my thoughtless question into this public commentary on his life. Beyond my contrition, however, was utter amazement that this man was only one year older than I was.

Women do not generally know their age in Afghanistan; usually referring to a nearest multiple of five years – 15, 20, 25 and so on until the older they get the less certain they are, even to the nearest five or ten years. Men usually have a better idea. It is an indictment on this society and the situation and value of women in Afghanistan. There was no hesitation from this man. He was fifty-five years old. Thinking generationally, I was the same as him. And yet, in every other way, he was the same as my father. It was an extremely disorientating observation.

'It was at this point, looking at a screen of faces in gallery mode — I'm pretty sure that you were one of them, Ruth — that my voice began to take on an unwanted tremolo, stalling every few words. I had to force it to re-start. It's weird to lose control of one's voice in such a way. I think that I minded less how I appeared to others in this state and more the interruption it created in what I was trying to say. The other thing of note was how it ambushed me. I had no inkling that this would happen. I was not even nervous before I began to speak. Maybe it was the memory of my dad that accessed my emotional deposit box while I was speaking and burst it open. Somehow I was able to continue, with Eva's hand, out of camera shot, alternatively patting and gripping my thigh. The words seem harmless now but at the time each was a trigger for sobbing:

> It was not so much that this man's life had been cut short by illness or accident: it had more been 'ground' short by a lifetime of deprivation and lack

of opportunity; having to use his muscle every day of his life in order to survive. And yet, his life story is just one amongst many, including the millions of 'ageless' women in Afghanistan.'

And me? I am still not sure how to talk of hope in the context of Afghanistan. We saw bleakness and suffering, rolling over people, endlessly, like breaking waves on a beach. So many Afghans were, and still are, caught in tragic situations where they have few or no choices. Like the women discovering the empty tomb, I am left bewildered and trembling.

'Now we have each spoken about our fathers, Ruth, I realise what I have in common with your father. He could not and would not talk of his experiences in the war. Whereas I have moved from not being able to speak about my time in Afghanistan to being able to do so, but not with any reliable control of my emotions. I suppose we gleaned something of what he felt through his letters and, of course, from that poem. But I am sorry that your dad never appeared to have had the opportunity to talk about what he experienced.'

I listened to Todd without saying anything. After all, he had done a lot of that when I recounted the events of my life. We sat silently. Eventually I spoke, 'Todd, it seems to me that our two stories have joined now to some extent, haven't they? If we're different, so much the better.

'But I do remember that Easter Sunday morning. I also recall your distress more recently. It was just a few weeks ago, when you shared something of the challenges facing your Afghan friends — the ones you are trying to help get to Australia. I think we were all startled on that first occasion because we had not appreciated what you experienced over there and how it impacted you. The second time we were more attuned to what you were saying, I think.'

'Yes, a physiotherapy colleague, and friend of seventeen years, was at that very time making the perilous escape, with his family, from Afghanistan for Pakistan. Before they left, he wrote to me — e mail allows this strange bridging of separate worlds. He told me how fearful he was of their imminent journey with all its dangers. When I shared this with the congregation, I guess that I was trying to offload some of the fear and anxiety that he had shared with me. So, while it may have irked me to break down once more as I spoke, it was less of a surprise. I have come to see that the burden of such sadness is not to be discarded or "gotten over". Instead, it is to be held and carried, on behalf of others, like it has some unknown part to play in a quest.'

'Going back then, can I ask you, Todd, what you intended in linking the story of the Afghan man and your father with the hope that Easter Sunday morning brings us? I didn't see it — the link, I mean'

'Well, I'm not sure I did either, Ruth. But I will say that I think hope is fundamental to our existence — on a level with food and water, I would say. And yet, maintaining it is as precarious at trying to hold water in cupped hands. It spills so easily. I'm not talking just about myself here. When others lose hope, like my Afghan friends in Pakistan waiting endlessly and fearfully for news of visas, then I seem to as well.

'I do keep looking for it though. Nowadays, I find it less in the recitation of creeds or affirmations of faith and more in the cracks of things; in things that are breaking down or damaged. Like returning green shoots in a blackened post bushfire landscape — they are so persistent, undeniable and "life-insisting". Believe it or not, I saw it in the compost the other day.

'To answer your question more directly, my encounter with the risen Jesus is also a confrontation with the choices I have been given. And one of those is to recognise and remember those who have little or no choice or voice.

'But you are right, Ruth. Our stories are closer than I would have ever expected, especially in what they have thrown back at us.'

'Well, Todd, we can both agree about the value of seeing what is in our shadows even when it brings us tears. I think it helps us see ourselves more truly in relation to others.

'Have you got time for a cup of tea? I have some carrot cake left over if you're interested.'

# Epilogue

*Truth on the ground is multiple, partial.*
*Fragments of it lie everywhere.*
— Rabbi Jonathan Sacks

Todd had almost finished writing up Ruth's story. The solitude and reflection of writing was familiar to him. Some years ago, as many as twenty, he had undertaken some post-graduate study. He had a pattern of working on his thesis in the mornings before heading off to do physiotherapy locum work in the afternoons. Between those two things, Todd would take a lunchtime walk to emerge from a world of ideas and be ready to enter one of practical problems.

One day, he had just crossed the road, starting out on such a walk, when he heard his nextdoor neighbour, Joe, call out to him. In retrospect, he knew that Joe had not just called out to say 'hello'. He had wanted to tell Todd something. Nevertheless, Todd treated it as the former, waved back and kept going. He should really have turned around given what he had seen the previous week. A week before, Todd had observed a highly unusual sight. Joe, who was well into his seventies, was on the oval doing sprints. Todd had been over on the other side of the reserve, several hundred metres away. He stopped walking and watched. He had never seen Joe run and was struck by his fluency and athleticism. Joe must have been quite a sprinter when he was young. He did not hold back now either. His body and spirit had teamed up for this moment. Joe's arms reached forward as if parting imaginary curtains in front of him, one arm and then the other, dipping into and then pulling back the air for propulsion. His curly silver hair bobbed in the wake of each raised knee stride. Todd saw a moment of freedom and joy.

A few days after that call-out on Todd's lunchtime walk, Joe went to hospital. He had decided to cease the dialysis he had been having for his renal failure and 'pull up stumps', as they say. He died not long after in an inevitable uremic coma. Dear Joe, who had once, without being asked or approached, had his towering pine trees cut down because their roots kept clogging Todd and Eva's drains. Joe, who never failed to greet their children as they walked past his house on their way to school. Joe, who had wanted that day to let Todd know of his intentions — he was sure of that now — Joe had passed on.

## EPILOGUE

Apart from the memories of good neighbour Joe, Todd continued to carry the image of him sprinting in his last days. Joe's sprints on the oval were, for Todd, an instance of an urge we all share at some point — to go back and remember something that we once held dear about ourselves. To touch once more the experience contained in that memory. To *feel* its truth.

In retreating to the garden, Todd had gone back, like Joe, to remember what his early Christian commitment had felt like. It was a call that had excited him and given great purpose. But that call had emanated from an understanding of God which had now, at least in part, fallen away. He had not only allowed that but thought it should happen, for lived experience and biblical doctrine do not always see eye to eye.

And while he still believed that he had followed both his heart and mind in this, the loss of *that* faith was not without costs. One of these was the loss of certainty or, at least, the promise of it. Sometimes, its absence felt like unresolved grief. Maybe this was what the 35ers had seen in him — another sadness, one that trails a lack of conviction.

These days, instead of certainty, what Todd held to be true was more often found as fragments or glimpses amid multiple, sometimes competing, accounts of life. It was, admittedly, not an appealing or compelling theology to try and articulate to others. And yet, it described the challenges Ruth had faced in determining the truth in her story. There, the truth had lain scattered in fragments rather than as one complete revelation. She had patiently picked up and held each newly discovered element of her life to the light. At age ninety-three, there was ongoing transformation with no use-by date. It was marvellous.

Todd's friendship with Ruth had refreshed his spirit as much as his retreat to the garden had. He could leave the garden now, and take its lessons with him. Unlike the evictions of the First Garden Story, this was not the departure of an exile. For he no longer carried the weight of all that knowledge as a kind of curse. He could venture forth with hands fumbling in pockets of hope, back to the tangle and jazz of community, to be with people like Ruth — and people unlike Ruth. Of the sadness in his shadow, and all that he had seen and done, of being a witness to the tragedy of others, and the weight of sorrow (theirs and his own), this was the life he had been given and he could welcome it, even be unharmed by it. It was less an accumulation of heavy baggage and more a transformation of the 'mix' that was composting in him — the ongoing regeneration of faith.

It has been a hard year. Evelyn's daughter Kaye passed away in April, and Reg's daughter Margaret, the one who started life as a 'blue baby', died late last year. It saddens me to be outliving the children of my siblings. And it is not just the children of my family either. Ian, whom I taught in Sunday

School as a six-year-old and was so proud of when he recited his lines for the Sunday School anniversary, despite his dyslexia, passed away this month from cancer. His camper trailer remains parked in my carport.

I still manage to live independently even though parts of me are wearing out. I had been sleeping in a chair for the last several months because of breathlessness. However, just recently, I received a bed via Veterans' Affairs. It can be tilted so that I can sleep more easily. It has been very helpful to me.

I have been having dreams lately where I am out with friends and find myself, at some point on our outing, all alone. My last dream of this kind was just after Queen Elizabeth died. I was visiting the Barossa with the Merry Widows, that small group of ours from church whose husbands had passed away. We passed a local football game and I wanted to stop and have a look. When, after watching some of the game, I turned around, they had all gone.

Jill — she always was William's favourite niece — is not only a confidant but brings William's mischievous humour back to me even now, especially in the tricky matter of how to sort out the house after I go. I do concede that it is a 'busy' place given that it has been occupied for so long by a person with an interest in history. (I have given her permission to use a skip.)

That reminds me of the impending local council hard rubbish collection. I needed an old mattress to be picked up and taken away. It was a bit of a rigmarole. The request had to be put in online. For goodness' sake! With my eyesight, that sort of thing only gets harder and harder. But friends from church helped me do that. I feel loved from so many directions.

This morning I rang the Sunday morning gardening show on ABC radio. I asked Sophie how I should manage my fig tree. It has grown far too large and I can't reach the figs. It has, like me, been around a while. William used to climb this same fig tree when he was a boy. Sophie prescribed a solid, even severe, pruning whilst warning that it might take a couple of years for it to fruit once more. My on-air reply was, 'I might not be here then!'

Naturally, they asked, 'Why?'

I told Sophie and host Peter that I was ninety-three years old. Well, for the next few minutes I became a subject of proclamation: 'Dear Listeners, you can be in your garden at any age.'

I look back on the dialogue of the past year and a half with Todd, and I am very grateful to now feel differently about my father. I still don't know the full truth about why he left

## EPILOGUE

Mum and us. The answer to that no longer seems so pressing. The bits and pieces concerning my family have been dug up, laid out for examination and reorganised in relation to each other. This reorganisation places my father and me in a better relationship than before. The image endures in me of him labouring, with disabled right arm, up that snaky rope ladder, carrying me out of the deep hold of the *Inverlass*. And I can now believe in the possibility that this — *finding me, holding me* — was his intention throughout the remainder of his life. For a large part of that time, I kept myself out of his reach. But eventually, I did search for him too. And we have met here. That comforts me.

I suppose I should have realised at the outset that this quest to better understand my family and our secrets would necessarily lead me back to myself. It was only when I started turning over the long-dormant leaf litter around the feet of my memories that I have come to better understand my family's secrets and the particular way I framed them over time. Now that they have had light and air, these secrets are no longer captive to stigma and shame. They have been released and offer me new ways of reconciling with my family and myself.

My back room, the place where I sit, and where Todd and I have spent so many hours talking, looks out onto my garden. The flower beds, fruit trees and vines are so close, and the windows so large and generous, that the garden seems to enter the room. It is a refreshing place. I love the morning sun that comes in at this time of year. It calls me to linger, to be still and quiet, even though there are other things I should be getting on with. I heed the call.

I think of my dearest William, and I realise, belatedly, that *not* sharing our concerns was not always the best course of action. It was part of how we all did things then. Oh, for all our wonderful companionship, the things we never talked through come to me strongly now, and I wish we had. We don't love perfectly, but thankfully, we don't have to. Grace assures me of that. We did so love each other. Our relationship just had its own particular course. I sit and think of all these things and the warmth of the morning sun is like a caress.

# Author's note

Pseudonyms have been used to protect the identities of several people. And yet we acknowledge that the specificity of times, places and events in this book will make the identity of the central character Ruth quite clear to many who know her (and the same holds true for Todd). So, why use pseudonyms? The answer is that the partners in dialogue – Ruth and Todd – discovered that the capacity for talking about long held family secrets is not the same for each person in a family. The process involves an acceptance of vulnerability, and in this, perspective counts. This realisation forms part of the story. The other reason we have maintained the use of pseudonyms is that it is helpful, at times, in achieving a sense of distance by which to better see persons and events from perspectives other than one's own.

# Sources

The primary informant regarding Port Adelaide and the church in Port Adelaide from the 1930s was 'Ruth' herself.

Below are other information sources followed by the chapter(s) in which they are used:

**Historical:**

1. John Couper-Smartt. *The History of a Commodious Harbor: Port Adelaide.* Adelaide: Wakefield Press, 2021. (Chapter One)
2. Ron Ritter. *Spanning Time and Tide: The Bridges of the Port Adelaide River.* Adelaide: Copyright Ronald. C. Ritter, 1996, p35. (Chapter One)
3. *Port Adelaide Centre Heritage Survey.* McDougall & Vines, Architectural and Heritage Consultants, Norwood, Adelaide SA. 1993. (Chapter Four)
4. *Narrative sketch of the foundation and early history of the Port Adelaide Congregation Church.* A booklet prepared from the original document written late in the 19th Century by Mr George P Hodge, senior son of the Rev Matthew Henry Hodge. (Chapter Four)

5. Potter Y. L. *Progress, Pubs and Piety: Port Adelaide 1836-1915*. Submitted in fulfilment of the requirements of the degree of Doctor of Philosophy. The University of Adelaide, 1999, pp338-339. (Chapter Four)

6. Mervyn Faggotter. Unpublished memories of his early life on Southern Yorke Peninsula, South Australia. (Chapters One and Eleven)

7. The poem copied by Ruth's father in WW1 is by Adam Lindsay Gordon. *To my Sister.* https://mypoeticside.com/show-classic-poem-11647 Accessed 26th August 2022. (Chapter Ten)

8. Trove - digital collections from Australian libraries, universities, museums, galleries and archives. https://trove.nla.gov.au/about/what-trove (Chapters Five, Eleven and Twelve)

9. Ancestry.com Free access weekend to the enlistment records of Australian servicemen. https://www.ancestry.com.au/cs/anzac-day Accessed 22nd April 2022. (Chapters Ten and Eleven)

## Theological:

1. The Bible verse from Genesis 3:23 which is used for the epigraph is from 'The Message' © 1993, 2002, 2018 by Eugene H. Peterson. All other bible verses are from 'The New International Version' ©1973, 1978, 1984, 2011 by Biblica, Inc.

2. Richard Rohr. *A Spring Within Us. A Year of Daily Meditations*. London: SPCK, 2018, p119 for the insight, 'if we do not transform our pain, we will most assuredly transmit it.' (Chapters Seven and Thirteen)

3. Howard Thurman. *When Knowledge Comes*. From: 'The Inward Journey'. Richmond, Indiana: Friends Uniting Press, (sixth printing) 2007, p16. (Chapter Seven)

4. Richard Rohr. *This is an Apocalypse*. Center for Action and Contemplation. Monday 6th April 2021. https://cac.org/daily-meditations/this-is-an-apocalypse-2021-04-26/ (Chapter Nine)

5. The story of the 'disgraced' Arizona priest comes from the National Public Radio website. https://www.npr.org/2022/02/15/1080829813/priest-resigns-baptisms accessed 14th August 2022. (Chapter Nine)

6. Richard Rohr. *Embracing Shadow and Light*. Center for Action and Contemplation, Monday 14th June 2021. https://cac.org/daily-meditations/embracing-shadow-and-light-2021-06-14/ (Chapter Thirteen)

7. David Tacey (ed.) *The Jung Reader. Part 1*. The Nature of the Psyche. Routledge, 2012, pp35-36. (Chapter Thirteen)

8. The story, 'My father and the Afghan man with painful knees' is taken from the blog: Ian and Anne in Afghanistan. Wordpress. https://anneandiane.wordpress.com/2011/02/ (Chapter Fifteen)

9. The inscription, 'Truth on the ground is multiple, partial. Fragments of it lie everywhere' is from Rabbi Jonathon Sacks, *The Dignity of Difference*. London: Bloomsbury Publishing, 2003, pp64. (Epilogue)

10. *What is the Second Naiveté? Engaging with Paul Ricoeur, Post-Critical Theology, and Progressive Christianity*. Presentation given by Linards Jansons to the teaching faculty of Australian Lutheran College, 30th October, 2014. https://www.academia.edu/14690650/What_is_the_Second_Naivet%C3%A9_Engaging_with_Paul_Ricoeur_Post_Critical_Theology_and_Progressive_Christianity (accessed 1st August 2022). (Epilogue)

11. Richard Rohr. *The Fisher King*. Center for Action and Contemplation, Monday 5th September 2022. https://cac.org/daily-meditations/the-fisher-king-2022-09-05/ (Epilogue).

# Acknowledgements

Thanks!

To Marianne Vreugdenhill and Barbara Washington for receiving and reading the earliest versions of this work with great patience and for staying the journey with me.

To my sister, Jane Edwards, who read a later draft and, with her usual perception, offered strategic comments and useable suggestions.

To Jessica Stewart from 'Your Second Draft' who did the copy editing and skilfully navigated her way through 'conversations within conversations' in the book so that those conversations could have a better shape and intelligibility.

To Marianne V (again) who proof read the final draft with a formidable eye for detail. And this was only equalled by her capacity to explain various grammatical and formatting issues and their conventions.

To Danica Gacesa McLean and Anne Edwards for the cover. Dani provided the artwork including advice and support from which Anne fashioned her wonderful material recreation of The Port. Anne also read chunks of text — on many occasions — answering my countless what-do-you-think questions with clarity and honesty.

To Rommie Corso from Hardshell Publishing for book design, typesetting, providing the hand drawn map of Ruth's 'Port Adelaide' and completing the final transformation of everything above into a book.

To my late parents Alan and Ruth. The memory of each of you came to me frequently in the writing of this book. You gave us so much. The extended family you have left behind continue to be incredibly grateful. We try to carry things forward. There is even an Alan and a Ruth in the names of two of your great grandchildren — great grandchildren that you never got to meet, much to your chagrin, Mum. And BTW Mum, your name was a unanimous choice for the heroine of this story.

**By the same author:**

The Second-Time Teacher:
Lessons from Afghanistan

For book orders and enquiries,
contact: anneandiane@hotmail.com

www.ingramcontent.com/pod-product-compliance
Lightning Source LLC
Chambersburg PA
CBHW030255010526
44107CB00053B/1717